Grades 1–3

Science
LESSONS FOR THE SMART BOARD™

Motivating, Interactive Lessons That Teach
Key Science Skills

SCHOLASTIC

New York ○ Toronto ○ London ○ Auckland ○ Sydney
New Delhi ○ Mexico City ○ Hong Kong ○ Buenos Aires

Teaching *Resources*

Authors: Sarah Carpenter, Karen Mawer, Jon Audain
Illustrators: Jim Peacock, Jenny Tulip, Theresa Tibbetts, Mark Brierley, Andy Keylock, Chris Saunderson, Ian Hunt
Editor: Maria L. Chang
Cover design: Brian LaRossa
Interior design: Grafica Inc.

CD-ROM developed in association with Q & D Multimedia.

Special thanks to Robin Hunt and Melissa Rugless of Scholastic Ltd.

SMART Board™ and Notebook™ are registered trademarks of SMART Technologies Inc.
Microsoft Office, Word, and Excel are either registered trademarks or trademarks of Microsoft Corporation in the United States and/or other countries.

All Flash activities designed and developed by Q & D Multimedia.

ISBN: 978-0-545-29047-0
Copyright © 2011 by Scholastic Inc.
All rights reserved.
Printed in the U.S.A.

2 3 4 5 6 7 8 9 10   40   18 17 16 15 14 13 12

Contents

Introduction

Interactive whiteboards are fast becoming the must-have resource in today's classroom as they allow teachers to facilitate children's learning in ways that were inconceivable a few years ago. The appropriate use of interactive whiteboards, whether used daily in the classroom or once a week in a computer lab, encourages active participation in lessons and increases children's determination to succeed. Interactive whiteboards make it easier for teachers to bring subjects across the curriculum to life in new and exciting ways.

What can an interactive whiteboard offer?

An interactive whiteboard allows teachers to do the same things they can on an ordinary whiteboard, such as drawing, writing, and erasing. However, the interactive whiteboard also offers many other possibilities, such as:

- saving any work created during a lesson;
- preparing as many pages as necessary;
- displaying any page within the Notebook™ file to review teaching and learning;
- adding scanned examples of children's work to a Notebook file;
- changing colors of shapes and backgrounds instantly;
- using simple templates and grids;
- linking Notebook files to spreadsheets, Web sites, and presentations.

Using an interactive whiteboard in the simple ways outlined above can enrich teaching and learning in a classroom, but that is only the beginning of the whiteboard's potential to educate and inspire.

For children, the interactive whiteboard provides the opportunity to share learning experiences, as lessons can be delivered with sound, still and moving images, and Web sites. Interactive whiteboards can be used to cater to the needs of all learning styles:

- Kinesthetic learners benefit from being able to physically manipulate images.
- Visual learners benefit from being able to watch videos, look at photographs, and see images being manipulated.
- Auditory learners benefit from being able to access audio resources, such as voice recordings and sound effects.

With a little preparation, all of these resource types could be integrated into one lesson—a feat that would have been almost impossible before the advent of the interactive whiteboard!

Access to an interactive whiteboard

In schools where children have limited access to interactive whiteboards, carefully planned lessons will help children get the most benefit from the board when it is available. As teachers become familiar with the interactive whiteboard, they will learn when to use it and, equally important, when not to use it!

In schools where there is unlimited access to interactive whiteboards, it is still important to plan the use of the board effectively. It should be used only in ways that will enhance or extend teaching and learning. Children still need to gain practical, first-hand experience in many areas. Some experiences cannot be recreated on interactive whiteboards, but others cannot be had without them. *Science Lessons for the SMART Board*™ offers both teachers and learners the most accessible and creative uses of this most valuable resource.

About the book

Adapted from Scholastic UK's best-selling 100 SMART Board Lessons series, *Science Lessons for the SMART Board*™ is designed to reflect best practice in using interactive whiteboards. It is also designed to support all teachers in using this valuable tool by providing lessons and other resources that can be used on the SMART Board with little or no preparation. These inspirational lessons meet the science standards and are perfect for all levels of experience.

This book is divided into the following six chapters:

- Health & the Human Body
- Plants & Animals
- Matter & Motion
- Light & Sound
- Magnetism & Electricity
- Rocks & Soil

Mini-Lessons

The mini-lessons have a consistent structure that includes:

- a **Getting Started** activity;
- a step-by-step **Mini-Lesson** plan;
- an **Independent Work** activity; and
- a **Wrap-Up** activity to round up the teaching and learning and identify any assessment opportunities.

Each mini-lesson identifies any resources required (including Notebook files that are provided on the CD-ROM, as well as reproducible activity pages) and lists the whiteboard tools that could be used in the mini-lesson.

The reproducible activity sheets toward the back of the book support the mini-lessons. These sheets provide opportunities for group or individual work to be completed away from the board, while linking to the context of the whiteboard lesson. They also provide opportunities for whole-class discussions in which children present their work.

What's on the CD-ROM?

The accompanying CD-ROM provides an extensive bank of Notebook files designed for use with the SMART Board. These support, and are supported by, the mini-lessons in this book. They can be annotated and saved for reference or for use with subsequent lessons; they can also be printed out. In addition to texts and images, a selection of Notebook files include the following types of files:

- **Embedded Microsoft Excel files:** The embedded files are launched from the Notebook file and will open in their native Microsoft application.
- **Embedded interactive files:** These include specially commissioned interactive files that will open in a new browser window within the Notebook environment.
- **Embedded audio files:** Some Notebook files contain buttons that play sounds.
- **"Build Your Own" file:** This contains a blank Notebook page with a bank of selected images and interactive tools from the Gallery, as well as specially commissioned images. It is supported by the mini-lesson plans in the book to help you build your own Notebook files.

The Notebook files

All of the Notebook files have a consistent structure as follows:

- **Title and objectives page—**Use this page to highlight the focus of the mini-lesson. You might also wish to refer to this page at certain times throughout the lesson or at the end of the lesson to assess whether the learning objective was achieved.
- **Getting Started activity—**This sets the context to the lesson and usually provides some key questions or learning points that will be addressed through the main activities.
- **Main activities—**These activities offer independent, collaborative group, or whole-class work. The activities draw on the full scope of Notebook software and the associated tools, as well as the SMART Board tools. "What to Do" boxes are also included in many of the prepared Notebook files. These appear as tabs in the top right-hand corner of the screen. To access these notes, simply pull out the tabs to reveal planning information, additional support, and key learning points.
- **Wrap-Up—**A whole-class activity or summary page is designed to review work done both at the board and away from the board. In many lessons, children are encouraged to present their work.

How to Use the CD-ROM

Setting up your screen for optimal use

It is best to view the Notebook pages at a screen display setting of 1280 x 1024 pixels. To alter the screen display, select Settings, then Control Panel from the Start menu. Next, double-click on the Display icon, then click on the Settings tab. Finally, adjust the Screen Area scroll bar to 1280 x 1024 pixels. Click on OK. (On the Mac, click on the apple icon and select System Preferences. Then click on Displays and select 1280 x 1024.)

If you prefer to use a screen display setting of 800 x 600 pixels, ensure that your Notebook view is set to "Page Width." To alter the view, launch Notebook and click on View. Go to Zoom and select the Page Width setting. If you use a screen display setting of 800 x 600 pixels, text in the prepared Notebook files may appear larger when you edit it on screen.

Getting started

The program should run automatically when you insert the CD-ROM into your CD drive. If it does not, use My Computer to browse to the contents of the CD-ROM and click on the Scholastic icon. (On the Mac, click on the Scholastic icon to start the program.)

Main menu

The Main menu divides the Notebook files by topic: Health & the Human Body; Plants & Animals; Matter & Motion; Light & Sound; Magnetism & Electricity; and Rocks & Soil. Clicking on the appropriate button for any of these options will take you to a separate Lessons menu. (See below for further information.) The "Build Your Own" file is also accessed through the Main menu.

Individual Notebook files or pages can be located using the search facility by keying in words (or part of words) from the resource titles in the Search box. Press Go to begin the search. This will bring up a list of the titles that match your search.

Lessons menu

Each Lessons menu provides all of the prepared Notebook files for each chapter of the book. Click on the buttons to open the Notebook files. Click on the Main menu button to return to the Main menu screen. (To alternate between the menus on the CD-ROM and other open applications, hold down the Alt key and press the Tab key to switch to the desired application.)

"Build Your Own" file

Click on this button to open a blank Notebook page and a collection of Gallery objects, which will be saved automatically into the My Content folder in the Gallery. (Under My Content, open the Year 3 Folder, then the Foundation folder to access the Gallery objects.) You only need to click on this button the first time you wish to access the "Build Your Own" file, as the Gallery objects will remain in the My Content folder on the computer on which the file was opened. To use the facility again, simply open a blank Notebook page and access the images and interactive resources from the same folder under My Content. If you are using the CD-ROM on a different computer, you will need to click on the "Build Your Own" button again.

Safety note: Avoid looking directly at the projector beam as it is potentially damaging to the eyes, and never leave children unsupervised when using the interactive whiteboard.

Connections to the Science Standards

The mini-lessons and activities in this book meet the following science standards*:

HEALTH & THE HUMAN BODY	
Body Parts	**Std 5, Lvl II, Benchmark 2:** Knows that living organisms have distinct structures and body systems that serve specific functions in growth, survival, and reproduction (e.g., various body structures for walking, flying, or swimming)
Food Groups; Keeping Healthy	**Std 5, Lvl I, Benchmark 1:** Knows the basic needs of plants and animals (e.g., air, water, nutrients, light or food, shelter) **Std 6, Lvl I, Benchmark 1:** Knows that plants and animals need certain resources for energy and growth (e.g., food, water, light, air)
How Are We Different?	**Std 4, Lvl I, Benchmark 2:** Knows that differences exist among individuals of the same kind of plant or animal **Std 7, Lvl I, Benchmark 2:** Knows that there are similarities and differences in the appearance and behavior of plants and animals
Healthy Teeth and Gums	**Std 5, Lvl II, Benchmark 2:** Knows that living organisms have distinct structures and body systems that serve specific functions in growth, survival, and reproduction (e.g., various body structures for walking, flying, or swimming)

PLANTS & ANIMALS	
Plants for Food	**Std 5, Lvl I, Benchmark 1:** Knows the basic needs of plants and animals (e.g., air, water, nutrients, light or food, shelter) **Std 6, Lvl I, Benchmark 1:** Knows that plants and animals need certain resources for energy and growth (e.g., food, water, light, air) **Std 6, Lvl II, Benchmark 1:** Knows the organization of simple food chains and food webs (e.g., green plants make their own food with sunlight, water, and air; some animals eat the plants; some animals eat the animals that eat the plants)
Plant Life Cycle	**Std 4, Lvl I, Benchmark 1:** Knows that plants and animals closely resemble their parents **Std 5, Lvl II, Benchmark 1:** Knows that plants and animals progress through life cycles of birth, growth and development, reproduction, and death; the details of these life cycles are different for different organisms
Investigation: Plant Leaves; Investigation: Water and Plants; Investigation: Light and Plants; Roots and Stems	**Std 5, Lvl I, Benchmark 1:** Knows the basic needs of plants and animals (e.g., air, water, nutrients, light or food, shelter) **Std 5, Lvl II, Benchmark 2:** Knows that living organisms have distinct structures and body systems that serve specific functions in growth, survival, and reproduction (e.g., various body structures for walking, flying, or swimming) **Std 6, Lvl I, Benchmark 1:** Knows that plants and animals need certain resources for energy and growth (e.g., food, water, light, air) **Std 12, Lvl I, Benchmark 1:** Knows that learning can come from careful observations and simple experiments **Std 12, Lvl I, Benchmark 2:** Knows that tools (e.g., thermometers, magnifiers, rulers, balances) can be used to gather information and extend the senses **Std 12, Lvl II, Benchmark 1:** Knows that scientific investigations involve asking and answering a question and comparing the answer to what scientists already know about the world **Std 12, Lvl II, Benchmark 3:** Plans and conducts simple investigations (e.g., formulates a testable question, plans a fair test, makes systematic observations, develops logical conclusions) **Std 12, Lvl II, Benchmark 4:** Uses appropriate tools and simple equipment (e.g., thermometers, magnifiers, etc.) to gather scientific data and extend the senses
Sorting Plants and Animals	**Std 5, Lvl II, Benchmark 2:** Knows that living organisms have distinct structures and body systems that serve specific functions in growth, survival, and reproduction (e.g., various body structures for walking, flying, or swimming) **Std 7, Lvl I, Benchmark 2:** Knows that there are similarities and differences in the appearance and behavior of plants and animals
Animals and Their Young; Animal Life Cycle	**Std 4, Lvl I, Benchmark 1:** Knows that plants and animals closely resemble their parents **Std 5, Lvl II, Benchmark 1:** Knows that plants and animals progress through life cycles of birth, growth and development, reproduction, and death; the details of these life cycles are different for different organisms

*Kendall, J. S., & Marzano, R. J. (2004). Content knowledge: A compendium of standards and benchmarks for K-12 education. Aurora, CO: Mid-continent Research for Education and Learning. Online database: http://www.mcrel.org/standards-benchmarks/

Categorizing Animals	**Std 4, Lvl I, Benchmark 2:** Knows that differences exist among individuals of the same kind of plant or animal
	Std 5, Lvl II, Benchmark 2: Knows that living organisms have distinct structures and body systems that serve specific functions in growth, survival, and reproduction (e.g., various body structures for walking, flying, or swimming)
	Std 7, Lvl I, Benchmark 2: Knows that there are similarities and differences in the appearance and behavior of plants and animals
What Animals Eat	**Std 5, Lvl I, Benchmark 1:** Knows the basic needs of plants and animals (e.g., air, water, nutrients, light or food, shelter)
	Std 6, Lvl I, Benchmark 1: Knows that plants and animals need certain resources for energy and growth (e.g., food, water, light, air)
	Std 12, Lvl II, Benchmark 2: Knows that scientists use different kinds of investigations (e.g., naturalistic observation of things or events, data collection, controlled experiments), depending on the questions they are trying to answer

MATTER & MOTION

Different Materials; Grouping Materials; Natural vs. Manmade	**Std 8, Lvl I, Benchmark 1:** Knows that different objects are made up of many different types of materials (e.g., cloth, paper, wood, metal) and have many different observable properties (e.g., color, size, shape, and weight)
Squashing, Bending, Twisting, Stretching	**Std 8, Lvl I, Benchmark 1:** Knows that different objects are made up of many different types of materials (e.g., cloth, paper, wood, metal) and have many different observable properties (e.g., color, size, shape, and weight)
	Std 8, Lvl I, Benchmark 2: Knows that things can be done to materials to change some of their properties (e.g., heating, freezing, mixing, cutting, dissolving, bending), but not all materials respond the same way to what is done to them
Heating Materials; Properties of Materials	**Std 8, Lvl I, Benchmark 2:** Knows that things can be done to materials to change some of their properties (e.g., heating, freezing, mixing, cutting, dissolving, bending), but not all materials respond the same way to what is done to them
	Std 9, Lvl I, Benchmark 2: Knows that heat can be produced in many ways (e.g., burning, rubbing, mixing substances together)
Investigation: Absorbency; Investigation: Stretchiness	**Std 8, Lvl I, Benchmark 1:** Knows that different objects are made up of many different types of materials (e.g., cloth, paper, wood, metal) and have many different observable properties (e.g., color, size, shape, and weight)
	Std 12, Lvl I, Benchmark 1: Knows that learning can come from careful observations and simple experiments
	Std 12, Lvl I, Benchmark 2: Knows that tools (e.g., thermometers, magnifiers, rulers, balances) can be used to gather information and extend the senses
	Std 12, Lvl II, Benchmark 1: Knows that scientific investigations involve asking and answering a question and comparing the answer to what scientists already know about the world
	Std 12, Lvl II, Benchmark 3: Plans and conducts simple investigations (e.g., formulates a testable question, plans a fair test, makes systematic observations, develops logical conclusions)
	Std 12, Lvl II, Benchmark 4: Uses appropriate tools and simple equipment (e.g., thermometers, magnifiers, etc.) to gather scientific data and extend the senses
Pushing and Pulling	**Std 10, Lvl I, Benchmark 4:** Knows that the position and motion of an object can be changed by pushing or pulling
What Makes It Move?	**Std 10, Lvl I, Benchmark 4:** Knows that the position and motion of an object can be changed by pushing or pulling
	Std 10, Lvl I, Benchmark 5: Knows that things move in many different ways (e.g., straight line, zigzag, vibration, circular motion)
	Std 10, Lvl II, Benchmark 5: Knows that when a force is applied to an object, the object either speeds up, slows down, or goes in a different direction
Types of Vehicles and Speed; Ramp Height and Speed	**Std 10, Lvl I, Benchmark 4:** Knows that the position and motion of an object can be changed by pushing or pulling
	Std 10, Lvl II, Benchmark 4: Knows that an object's motion can be described by tracing and measuring its position over time
	Std 10, Lvl II, Benchmark 5: Knows that when a force is applied to an object, the object either speeds up, slows down, or goes in a different direction
	Std 10, Lvl II, Benchmark 6: Knows the relationship between the strength of a force and its effect on an object (e.g., the greater the force, the greater the change in motion; the more massive the object, the smaller the effect of a given force)

LIGHT & SOUND

Sources of Light	**Std 9, Lvl I, Benchmark 1:** Knows that the Sun supplies heat and light to Earth
	Std 9, Lvl II, Benchmark 3: Knows that light can be reflected, refracted, or absorbed
How Shadows Form	**Std 9, Lvl I, Benchmark 5:** Knows that light travels in a straight line until it strikes an object
	Std 9, Lvl II, Benchmark 3: Knows that light can be reflected, refracted, or absorbed
Investigation: Shadow Length	**Std 3, Lvl I, Benchmark 1:** Knows basic patterns of the Sun and Moon (e.g., the Sun appears every day and the Moon appears sometimes at night and sometimes during the day; the Sun and Moon appear to move from east to west across the sky; the Sun's position in the sky changes through the seasons)
	Std 9, Lvl I, Benchmark 1: Knows that the Sun supplies heat and light to Earth
	Std 12, Lvl I, Benchmark 1: Knows that learning can come from careful observations and simple experiments
	Std 12, Lvl I, Benchmark 2: Knows that tools (e.g., thermometers, magnifiers, rulers, balances) can be used to gather information and extend the senses
	Std 12, Lvl II, Benchmark 3: Plans and conducts simple investigations (e.g., formulates a testable question, plans a fair test, makes systematic observations, develops logical conclusions)
	Std 12, Lvl II, Benchmark 4: Uses appropriate tools and simple equipment (e.g., thermometers, magnifiers, etc.) to gather scientific data and extend the senses
Using Shadows to Tell Time	**Std 3, Lvl I, Benchmark 1:** Knows basic patterns of the Sun and Moon (e.g., the Sun appears every day and the Moon appears sometimes at night and sometimes during the day; the Sun and Moon appear to move from east to west across the sky; the Sun's position in the sky changes through the seasons)
	Std 9, Lvl I, Benchmark 1: Knows that the Sun supplies heat and light to Earth
Opaque vs. Transparent	**Std 9, Lvl I, Benchmark 5:** Knows that light travels in a straight line until it strikes an object
	Std 9, Lvl II, Benchmark 3: Knows that light can be reflected, refracted, or absorbed
Sounds Around Us; Making Sounds	**Std 9, Lvl I, Benchmark 4:** Knows that sound is produced by vibrating objects

MAGNETISM & ELECTRICITY

Properties of Magnets	**Std 10, Lvl I, Benchmark 1:** Knows that magnets can be used to make some things move without being touched
	Std 10, Lvl I, Benchmark 2: Knows that things near the Earth fall to the ground unless something holds them up
	Std 10, Lvl II, Benchmark 1: Knows that magnets attract and repel each other and attract certain kinds of materials (e.g., iron, steel)
	Std 10, Lvl II, Benchmark 2: Knows that the Earth's gravity pulls any object toward it without touching it
Magnetic Materials	**Std 10, Lvl I, Benchmark 1:** Knows that magnets can be used to make some things move without being touched
	Std 10, Lvl II, Benchmark 1: Knows that magnets attract and repel each other and attract certain kinds of materials (e.g., iron, steel)
What Does Electricity Do?; Dangers of Electricity; Building a Circuit; Testing Circuits	**Std 9, Lvl I, Benchmark 3:** Knows that electricity in circuits can produce light, heat, sound, and magnetic effects

ROCKS & SOIL

Rocks Everywhere!	**Std 2, Lvl I, Benchmark 1:** Knows that Earth materials consist of solid rocks, soils, liquid water, and the gases of the atmosphere
	Std 2, Lvl I, Benchmark 2: Knows that rocks come in many different shapes and sizes (e.g., boulders, pebbles, sand)
	Std 2, Lvl II, Benchmark 3: Knows that rock is composed of different combinations of minerals
Soils; Investigation: Water Flow	**Std 2, Lvl I, Benchmark 1:** Knows that Earth materials consist of solid rocks, soils, liquid water, and the gases of the atmosphere
	Std 2, Lvl I, Benchmark 2: Knows that rocks come in many different shapes and sizes (e.g., boulders, pebbles, sand)
	Std 2, Lvl II, Benchmark 4: Knows the composition and properties of soil (e.g., components of soil such as weathered rock, living organisms, products of plants and animals; properties of soil such as color, texture, capacity to retain water, ability to support plant growth)

Body Parts

Learning objectives

- To know that humans have bodies with similar parts.
- To be able to name parts of the human body.

Resources

- "Body Parts" Notebook file
- "Label the Body Parts" (p. 55)
- sticky notes

Whiteboard tools

- Pen tray
- Select tool
- Screen Shade
- Spotlight tool

Getting Started

Open page 2 of the "Body Parts" Notebook file and sing "Head, Shoulders, Knees and Toes," ensuring that children point to the correct body parts as they sing along. Ask them to tell you what the song is about. Introduce the phrase *body parts*.

Sing the song a second time, but this time tell children not to say the word *head*, but just to touch their heads instead. For each verse thereafter, add another body part that children should touch instead of saying the word out loud.

Mini-Lesson

1. Go to page 3 of the Notebook file. Slowly move the Screen Shade to reveal the body part image, asking children to identify it. Repeat this for pages 4 to 12, using a pen from the Pen tray to write the name of the body part on each page.

2. Go to page 13. Ask children to help you write a list of body parts in preparation for their Independent Work.

3. Play "Simon Says," using the list of body parts (for example, *Simon says, "Touch your knee."*)

Independent Work

Hand out copies of "Label the Body Parts" (p. 55). Ask children to label the body, choosing the appropriate word from the word bank at the bottom of the sheet.

You could give less-confident learners sticky notes with the names of the body parts to stick onto themselves (or onto a large drawing of a child). Give more-confident learners an adapted sheet with the word bank removed.

Wrap-Up

Enable the Spotlight tool, choose the circle, and make it smaller. Go to page 14 of the Notebook file and move the spotlight around the image of the body, asking children to name the body parts that they can identify. Use a pen from the Pen tray to write relevant words to label the body. Write any further labels that children may suggest. Ensure that children understand that these body parts are common to all humans.

Food Groups

Learning objectives
- To know that there are many different foods.
- To record information in drawings and charts.
- To know that we eat different kinds of food.
- To be able to collect information and present the results in a bar graph.

Resources
- "Food Groups" Notebook file
- "Food Diary" (p. 56)
- "Food Groups" (p. 57)
- graph paper (optional)

Whiteboard tools
- Pen tray
- Select tool
- Highlighter pen
- Dual Page Display

Before You Start
A few days prior to the lesson, ask children, as homework, to keep a food diary for one day and return it for the lesson. Supply them with a copy of "Food Diary" (p. 56).

Getting Started
Ask children to look at their food diaries (see Before You Start) and talk with them about what they eat. Find out what they already know about food, particularly with regard to staying healthy. Ask: *What would happen if we didn't eat or drink? What would happen if we ate only one sort of food? What do you understand by the term* healthy? Record children's responses on page 2 of the "Food Groups" Notebook file.

Mini-Lesson
1. Consider the pull-out question on page 2 of the Notebook file and then look at page 3 with children. Check that they know what the different foods are.

2. Explain that different types of food do different jobs in our bodies and that this is why it is important to eat a variety of foods to remain healthy.

3. Support children in sorting the food pictures into the correct food groups. Talk about their decisions and give definitions for any new vocabulary.

4. Show children Jack's food diary on page 4. Ask them to identify the food groups that the foods in the diary belong to.

5. Go to page 5 and tell children that you will be working together to use the tally chart to sort the food in Jack's diary into the five food groups. Refer back to page 4 to look at what Jack ate and record the results in the tally chart on page 5. (Click on the Dual Page Display icon to display both pages side-by-side.) Highlight the foods on page 4 as they are recorded in the tally chart. Print out the results on page 5.

6. Go to page 6. Using the printout of page 5, show children how to drag and drop the colored boxes from the bottom of the page into the appropriate place on the bar graph to illustrate the tally chart data (about Jack's food).

Independent Work
Give each child a copy of "Food Groups" (p. 57). Ask children to transfer the information from their own food diaries onto the tally chart. Provide plenty of support at this stage, as some foods (such as frozen dinners) can be difficult to classify into one particular group. Ask children to use tally chart data to create a bar graph using the template on the sheet.

Wrap-Up
Look at the bar graph created earlier on page 6 of the Notebook file. Ask children what they think it shows about Jack's diet. Ask questions about the chart such as: *Is Jack eating a healthy diet? Has Jack eaten five portions of fruits and vegetables? Is Jack a vegetarian?* Write children's responses on page 7. Give children an opportunity to evaluate their own eating habits with a partner. Ask some children to give feedback on their discussions to the rest of the class.

Keeping Healthy

- To understand that humans need water and food to stay alive.
- To understand that humans need exercise to stay healthy.
- To make and record observations and make simple comparisons.

Resources
- "Keeping Healthy" Notebook file
- posters about healthy living
- outdoor space
- plain paper
- felt-tipped pens

Whiteboard tools
- Pen tray
- Select tool

Getting Started

Ask children to talk with a partner about what they think humans need to do to keep healthy. Listen to some of their ideas and then open the "Keeping Healthy" Notebook file. Show the list of statements on page 2. Ask children to decide which statements belong in the box. Talk about their ideas and correct any misconceptions.

Mini-Lesson

1. Ask children to sit quietly for one minute and consider how their bodies feel when they are at rest. Record key words on page 3.

2. Take children into the playground and ask them to play an active game for a few minutes. Afterwards, ask: *How do your bodies feel now?*

3. Encourage children to think about what changes have occurred in their bodies, and why these may have happened. Record a few sentences on page 3.

4. Alternatively, instead of recording ideas as a class on the SMART Board, give children the opportunity to record individually how they felt before and after exercising, using key words and drawings.

5. Ask children to consider the kinds of exercise they do. Ensure that they understand that there are many alternative ways to exercise. Talk about the benefits of exercise.

6. If possible, show some posters promoting healthy living, particularly those relating to exercise. Talk about their layout and the message they portray.

7. There is an example of a simple poster on page 4 of the Notebook file. The poster labels are mixed up; invite children to drag them to the correct position.

Independent Work

Give children a plain piece of paper and some felt-tipped pens. Have them each create a poster promoting the benefits of exercise to other children in the school. Encourage children to talk to a partner about the message they want to get across on their poster. Make sure children consider the layout and content of the poster carefully before they begin—for example, large, bold lettering, using all of the page and appropriate drawings to support the message.

Wrap-Up

Scan samples of children's posters and upload the scanned images by selecting Insert, then Picture File, and browsing to where you have saved the images. Display the posters on page 5 of the Notebook file and invite the class to comment on them. Ask: *What message is the poster giving? Does it motivate you to do some exercise?* Encourage positive comments from children. Ask children to review with a partner what humans need to do to stay healthy. Assess how far their learning has progressed during the lesson.

How Are We Different?

Learning objectives

- To know that some differences among children can be measured.
- To measure hand span in standard units of length, make comparisons, and present measurements in a bar graph.
- To raise questions about differences among children, test them, and decide whether predictions were correct.

Resources

- "How Are We Different?" Notebook file
- "Investigating Differences," Parts 1 and 2 (pp. 58–59)
- measuring tools
- paper
- pencils
- rulers
- scissors

Whiteboard tools

- Pen tray
- Select tool
- On-screen Keyboard

(Microsoft Excel is required to view the embedded spreadsheet in the Notebook file.)

Getting Started

Show children what is meant by the term *hand span*. Ask them to predict which child will have the largest hand span. Use page 2 of the "How Are We Different?" Notebook file to demonstrate how to measure a hand span. Ask children to draw around one of their hands on a sheet of paper, then cut out the paper hands and use rulers to measure the span (in centimeters). Tell them to write their hand-span measurements on the paper hands. Find out who has the largest hand span.

Mini-Lesson

1. Wonder aloud whether the tallest person in the class has the largest hand span. Look at the first question on page 3 of the Notebook file. Ask: *How can we find out whether the tallest person in the class has the largest hand span?* Write children's ideas in the first box on page 4. Then consider the other two questions and write their ideas in the second and third boxes.

2. Open the spreadsheet on page 5 and show children the worksheet labeled "Hand span v height."

3. Choose ten children and measure their heights (in centimeters). Write the heights on cards that the children can hold in front of them. Ask them to stand in order from shortest to tallest. Use the On-screen Keyboard to enter the ten children's names (from shortest to tallest) and corresponding heights into the spreadsheet. A bar chart of children's heights will appear.

4. Now enter the same children's hand-span measurements into the spreadsheet next to their heights. A bar chart of children's hand spans will appear.

5. Look at the two bar charts with children and ask questions about the charts.

6. Ask children to answer the original question (whether or not the person with the largest hand span is also the tallest person). Ask them to explain how the bar chart shows them this.

7. Return to page 5 and explain that children will answer the other two questions.

Independent Work

Have children work in groups of five and challenge them to answer the second question (whether the tallest children have the longest feet). Supply paper, measuring tools, and scissors for children. Ask them to take accurate measurements of foot length and height. Supply each child with a copy of "Investigating Differences," Parts 1 and 2 (pp. 58–59). Ask the group to share their measurements to complete the sheets. Encourage children to use their results to find an answer. Arrange children into mixed-ability groups to support the less-confident learners.

Wrap-Up

Share the results from each group's investigation. Using the Microsoft Excel file link on page 5 of the Notebook file, enter the results of ten children's measurements into the worksheet labeled "Foot length v height" and make a final conclusion.

Ask children to predict the answer to the third question based on what they have learned so far. Ask ten children for their hand span and their foot length. Enter these into the "Hand span v foot length" tab on the spreadsheet to form a conclusion. Ask children to suggest other questions that could be investigated involving differences among themselves. Use page 6 for notes.

Healthy Teeth and Gums

Learning objectives
- To understand that healthy teeth need healthy gums.
- To know that some foods can be damaging to our teeth.

Resources
- "Healthy Teeth and Gums" Notebook file
- paper
- drawing materials

Whiteboard tools
- Pen tray
- Select tool
- Fill Color tool

Getting Started

Display page 2 of the "Healthy Teeth and Gums" Notebook file. Ask children about their midday snacks and discuss how healthful they think the snacks are. Discuss the fact that what children eat also directly affects the health of their teeth and gums. Ask children how many times a day they brush their teeth and why they think it is important. Explain that brushing keeps their gums healthy. Survey how many children brush their teeth after sugary snacks and drinks.

Mini-Lesson

1. Go to page 3 of the Notebook file. Drag the labels out of the box at the bottom of the page. Complete the diagram and review any prior work on the names and functions of the teeth. Use the Fill Color tool to fill the bottom of the boxes with white to check answers.

2. Go to page 4 and tell children that they will read about what healthy and unhealthy teeth and gums look like. Display page 5 and discuss in detail the descriptions of healthy and unhealthy teeth and gums.

3. Engage children in a discussion about what might lead to unhealthy teeth and gums, such as not brushing regularly or eating certain foods or drinks. Do not, at this stage, mention sugar. Explain that some foods damage your teeth and gums and some foods protect and strengthen them.

4. Display page 6 and ask children to sort the food into two groups and discuss their reasons.

5. Guide children to understand that foods like vegetables, cheese, and milk are good for healthy teeth and gums. Ask children why these foods are good (for example, milk and cheese contain calcium).

6. Discuss whether or not children think the other foods are bad for your teeth and what these foods have in common (high levels of sugar). Explain that sugar damages the teeth and gums, making sugary snacks at recess inappropriate, as children don't brush their teeth afterwards.

Independent Work

Challenge children to design a poster persuading other children in the school to eat snacks that are good for their teeth. Tell them that their posters must use pictures, slogans, and other persuasive writing and must inform their audience about the dangers of sugary snacks. Encourage them to plan first and to use a simple, clear, and bold design.

Wrap-Up

Ask children to present their posters. Scan a selection of their work to display on page 7 of the Notebook file. Upload scanned posters by selecting Insert, then Picture File, and browsing to where you have saved the images.

Plants for Food

- To know that plants provide food for humans.

Resources
- "Plants for Food" Notebook file
- photographs and real examples of plants that provide food for humans (for example, fruits, vegetables, and cereals)
- recipe for vegetable soup, vegetable salad, or fruit salad, and the ingredients and utensils to make it

Safety Note: Seek permission from parents or guardians before tasting food in class.

Whiteboard tools
- Pen tray
- Select tool

Getting Started

Engage children in a discussion about what they know about plants. Ask: *Why do we grow plants?* Write their suggestions on page 2 of the "Plants for Food" Notebook file. If the answer "to provide food for humans" does not come up, show children a photograph of a plant that provides food, such as a tomato plant or an apple tree. Ask them to suggest other plants that are grown to provide food for humans.

Go to page 3 of the Notebook file and invite children to match up the food with the plants by selecting the images and dragging them to the appropriate position on the page.

Mini-Lesson

1. Show children some real examples of plants that are grown to provide humans with food. Allow them to explore these plants and discuss what they see, smell, and feel. If possible, let them taste the edible parts. (**Safety note:** Check for food allergies and intolerances, such as wheat intolerance, before doing this.)

2. Ensure that children know the names of the different plants and, where applicable, how the plants are made ready to eat. Discuss with them which part of each plant is eaten: root, stem, leaf, flower, fruit, or seed.

3. Look again at page 3 of the Notebook file and discuss where each food item grows. Discuss any different food items that you've looked at and show children where each of these food items grows.

Independent Work

Have one or two groups of children, with the assistance of an adult, make a vegetable salad, a fruit salad, or a vegetable soup. Discuss with children which part of each plant is eaten and how it is prepared for eating. Other children can draw pictures of the food that was used during the Mini-Lesson and state which part of the plant is eaten. If possible, show children who are uncertain the whole plant in context: for example, show carrots being pulled from the ground, to illustrate that it is the root that we eat.

More-confident learners could consider some food plants that are harder to categorize (for example, tomatoes and cucumbers are fruits but are used like vegetables).

Wrap-Up

Go to page 4 of the Notebook file. Ask a volunteer to drag the pictures into the correct column. Encourage children to add the names of any other plants they have been drawing or cooking with into the different groups. Can they explain how they know which part of the plant is eaten? Can they add further edible plants to the table? Go to page 5 and ask why it is important for humans to grow plants. Note down children's responses on the page. Ask children what they have learned in this lesson and write their conclusions on page 6.

Plant Life Cycle

Learning objectives
- To know that flowering plants produce seeds.
- To know that seeds produce new plants.

Resources
- "Plant Life Cycle" Notebook file
- an apple
- a variety of flowers and fruits with seeds inside them
- soil and small plant pots
- stickers
- a flowering plant in a pot
- a dandelion in its various stages
- magnifying glasses

Safety note: Make sure you are aware of any children's allergies and check a plant guide to ensure none of the plants are poisonous.

Whiteboard tools
- Pen tray
- Select tool

Getting Started

Show children a flowering plant in a pot and ask them to explain to a partner where they think the plant came from. Encourage them to add as much detail to their explanations as possible. For example, if children suggest that the plant grew from a seed, ask them where the seed came from. Make note of their responses on page 2 of the "Plant Life Cycle" Notebook file.

Mini-Lesson

1. Show children an apple and ask them where they think it came from.

2. Look at page 3 of the Notebook file. Invite children to drag and drop the labels describing the stages of an apple's life cycle into place.

3. Ask children to decide where they think you should begin to read the information. Elicit that there is no correct starting point and that is why it is displayed as a cyclical diagram.

4. Share the life cycle of an apple with children, talking about every stage in detail.

5. Move on to page 4. Ask children to label the parts of the plant, dragging and dropping the labels from the red box into the appropriate positions.

6. Ask children to try to describe the life cycle of a dandelion to a partner. Listen to their ideas and then explain the life cycle, showing children real dandelions at the different stages, if possible.

Independent Work

Give each group a variety of different flowers and fruits with seeds on or inside them. Ask children to have a close look at them. Challenge children to find and harvest the seeds from each of the flowers and fruits. Give them the opportunity to look closely at the seeds with magnifying glasses. Ensure that children know not to eat the seeds and be aware of any allergies that they may have. Give children some soil, plant pots, and stickers and ask them to plant the seeds into the pots and label them. Help them plant the seeds correctly. Ask children to make predictions about what will happen next.

Wrap-Up

Talk with children about what they might expect to happen to their seeds now that they have been planted. Ask: *Will the seeds grow if we just leave them on the windowsill? What do the seeds need to grow into healthy plants?* Assess children's understanding. Challenge children to say what type of plant their seeds will grow into to ensure that they understand the concept that the seed can only grow into the same species of plant that it came from. Write children's ideas on page 5 of the Notebook file to provide a record that you can return to.

Investigation: Plant Leaves

Learning objectives

- To make careful observations and take measurements of plants growing.
- To use simple tools to measure the height of plants in standard measures.
- To use results to draw conclusions.
- To understand that plants need leaves in order to grow well.

Resources

- "Investigation: Plant Leaves" Notebook file
- "Plant Investigations" (p. 60)
- two similar plants of the same species (for example, geranium)
- rulers
- water
- measuring cups

Whiteboard tools

- Pen tray
- Select tool

Getting Started

Use page 2 of the "Investigation: Plant Leaves" Notebook file to discuss what factors affect the healthy growth of plants (for example, water, temperature, or light). Label the diagram together. Discuss children's experiences of planting, growing, and looking after plants at home. Show them the plants and identify the leaves, stem, and flowers. Draw out their knowledge of the functions of these parts and those of any unseen parts, such as the roots.

Mini-Lesson

1. Discuss with children how they could find out whether plants need leaves in order to grow well. Help them understand how removing the leaves from one plant, and then keeping both plants in the same place and watering them the same amount, would provide a fair comparison.

2. On page 3 of the Notebook file, write down a suitable location for the plants, how much water they will be given and when, and what children will need to measure and record.

3. Invite children to record this information on the top box of their copies of "Plant Investigations" (p. 60).

4. Demonstrate how to measure the plant accurately from the top of the soil next to the stem, to the top of the plant.

Independent Work

Over a period of a few weeks, have children water and measure the plants according to an agreed-upon plan. On page 4 of the Notebook file, use a Pen from the Pen tray to write down the dates and measurements as the investigation progresses. Remember to save the Notebook file each time. Leave a printout of page 4 beside the plants to remind children of the information that needs to be recorded. Monitor the investigation so that it remains fair, by ensuring that children measure heights and amount of water accurately.

Support less-confident learners by discussing how the fair testing will help produce more accurate results. Challenge more-confident learners by asking them to predict the outcome of the investigation and to explore their ideas about why leaves would affect growth.

Wrap-Up

Display the recorded measurements on page 4 of the Notebook file and discuss the results. Establish that plants need leaves to grow well. Ask children for their ideas about why this is so. Some children may have a basic awareness of the function of leaves and the oxygen/carbon dioxide transfer involved in photosynthesis. Write the conclusion at the bottom of page 4. As a precursor to other possible investigations, ask children to suggest other factors that might influence growth, such as light, water, and temperature.

Investigation: Water and Plants

Learning objectives

- To know that plants need water, but not unlimited water, for healthy growth.
- To use simple tools to measure a volume of water correctly.
- To use simple tools to measure the height of the plant.

Resources

- "Investigation: Water and Plants" Notebook file
- "Plant Investigations" (p. 60)
- a minimum of four containers of bean seedlings
- rulers
- water
- measuring cups or syringes suitable for small quantities
- measuring spoons (5ml)

Whiteboard tools

- Pen tray
- Select tool

Getting Started

Review any prior knowledge of factors that affect the healthy growth of plants (for example, the number of leaves, temperature, or light). Discuss children's experiences of watering plants at home. Many children will have experienced plants dying due to lack of water, but they may be less familiar with over-watering. Look at some plant care labels to find out information about caring for them.

Mini-Lesson

1. Display page 2 of the "Investigation: Water and Plants" Notebook file and discuss what will happen to the three plants. Ask children: *Do you think the more water plants are given, the better they will grow?* (Press the seedlings to see the results.)

2. Discuss how children could find out how much water bean seedlings need in order to grow well. Elicit how to provide a fair comparison: by changing the amount of water each seedling is given (while keeping other conditions, such as light and temperature, the same) and regularly measuring the height of each plant.

3. Decide how much each seedling will be watered (5ml, 20ml, or 50ml per day). Establish that one seedling should not be watered at all to provide further comparison.

4. On page 3, write down a suitable location for the plants, how much water each one will be given and when, and what children will need to measure and record.

5. Ask children to record this information on the middle box of their copies of "Plant Investigations" (p. 60).

6. Demonstrate how to measure the seedling accurately from the top of the soil to the top of the plant and how to fill the measuring cup accurately with small quantities of water.

Independent Work

Organize children to water and measure each plant on a regular basis. On page 4 of the Notebook file, use a Pen from the Pen tray to write down the dates and measurements as the investigation progresses. Remember to save the Notebook file each time. Leave a printout of page 4 by the plants to remind children of what information needs to be recorded. Monitor the investigation to check that it remains fair by ensuring accurate measuring.

Support less-confident learners by discussing how fair testing will help produce more accurate results. Challenge more-confident learners by asking them to predict the outcome of the investigation and by exploring their ideas about how the amount of watering will affect growth.

Wrap-Up

Display the recorded measurements on page 4 of the Notebook file and discuss what the results show. Establish that plants need water, but not unlimited water, for healthy growth. (Their root systems require air as well as water. An over-watered plant drowns because of lack of oxygen from the soil.) Write the conclusion on page 4. As a precursor to other possible investigations, ask children to suggest other factors that might influence growth (such as number of leaves, light, and temperature).

Investigation: Light and Plants

Learning objectives
- To know that plants need light for healthy growth.
- To ask questions about the growth of plants.

Resources
- "Investigation: Light and Plants" Notebook file
- "Plant Investigations" (p. 60)
- minimum of two containers of bean seedlings
- rulers
- water
- measuring cups, syringes, or spoons (5ml) suitable for small quantities

Whiteboard tool
- Pen tray

Getting Started
Recap any previous work on factors that affect the healthy growth of plants (for example, the number of leaves, water, or temperature).

Mini-Lesson
1. Open the "Investigation: Light and Plants" Notebook file and go to page 2. Use this page to discuss what happens when a large object, such as a tent, is left on top of grass for a long time (for example, it isn't as green as the surrounding grass). Discuss why this might happen; possible causes include lack of light.

2. Discuss together how children could find out how important light is to the healthy growth of plants. Keeping two similar plants in separate light and dark locations, while watering them equally, would provide a fair comparison.

3. Decide how much each seedling will be watered and what needs to be recorded (a physical description of the plant and its height) and how often.

4. Record this information on page 3, along with suitable locations for the plants.

5. Ask children to record this information on the bottom box of their own copies of "Plant Investigations" (p. 60).

6. Demonstrate how to accurately measure the seedling from the top of the soil to the top of the plant and how to precisely fill the measuring tools with small quantities of water.

Independent Work
Every few days, have children water and measure each plant according to an agreed-upon plan. On page 4 of the Notebook file, use a Pen from the Pen tray to write down the dates and measurements as the investigation progresses. Remember to save the data file each time. Monitor that the investigation remains fair by ensuring that children measure heights and volumes accurately.

Support less-confident learners by discussing how the fair testing will help produce more accurate results. Challenge more-confident learners by asking them to predict the outcome of the investigation and to explore their ideas about how the amount of light will affect growth.

Wrap-Up
Display and discuss what the recorded measurements on page 4 show. Establish that plants need light for healthy growth. Plants need energy from sunlight to *photosynthesize* (change carbon dioxide and water into glucose and oxygen). Write the conclusion at the bottom of page 4. (Without light, plants eventually become long, yellow, and spindly.) Discuss why plants don't start dying at night. (Plants make enough energy from sunshine to last them through the night, and through lots of cloudy days.) Ask children to predict what would happen if the plant that has been kept in the dark were put back into the light for a few days. As a precursor to other possible investigations, ask children to suggest other factors that might influence growth, such as the number of leaves, water, and temperature.

Roots and Stems

Learning objectives

- To know that water is taken in through the roots.
- To understand that water is transported through the stem to other parts of the plant.
- To make careful observations and present these using drawings.
- To explain observations.

Resources

- "Roots and Stems" Notebook file
- "Stem Observation" (p. 61)
- a potted plant with a clump of overgrown roots
- a complete head of celery
- cut celery stems with leaves
- water
- bright food coloring
- suitable containers
- plastic knives
- magnifying glasses
- colored pencils
- paper or science notebook

Whiteboard tools

- Pen tray
- Select tool
- Area Capture tool

Getting Started

Display the learning objective on page 1 of the "Roots and Stems" Notebook file. Show children the roots of a potted plant. Ask what has happened and what they would expect to see if the roots were in a larger pot. (The roots would spread out.) Guide children to recognize that roots spread out in order to take in water from the surrounding soil more easily. Use page 2 to emphasize this point.

Mini-Lesson

1. Explain to children that they will be investigating what happens to the water that is taken in by roots.

2. Show children a whole head of celery and identify the stems, leaves, and where the roots used to be.

Independent Work

Ask children to examine the cut end of the stems closely with a magnifying glass, describing their observations. Hand out copies of the "Stem Observation" sheet (p. 61). Ask children to place the stems upright, with the cut end down, in a shallow amount of colored liquid (water with food coloring) in a container. Invite them to draw the setup in black and white, showing the position of the colored water using a colored pencil. After a few hours, ask children to observe the stems closely and to redraw the setup and the position of the colored water. Repeat a final time a few hours later.

Check the stems periodically until you can see evidence of color in the veins of the celery leaves. Help children cut the stems several centimeters above the end to reveal a cross-section of the stem. Ask children to observe the cut stem carefully and identify where the dye has traveled up. Now help them cut the stems a few centimeters higher and repeat, following the path of the dye up the stem. Invite children to examine the leaves with a magnifying glass to look for evidence of dye entering the veins of the leaves.

Support less-confident learners as they observe the experiment and provide help in accurately drawing the setup. Challenge more-confident learners by asking them to predict the outcome of the investigation.

Wrap-Up

Discuss children's observations and recordings, drawing out evidence that water has traveled up the stem toward and into the leaves. Annotate their ideas on page 3 of the Notebook file. Click on the "Roots and Stems" interactive activity to help children explain their observations by dragging the labels to their correct positions around the diagram. Explain that the water is transported to the leaves to aid the healthy growth of the plant. (It is required for photosynthesis.) Print out the correctly labeled diagram. Alternatively, use the Area Capture tool to take a snapshot of the completed activity and save the diagram into a new Notebook page.

Sorting Plants and Animals

Learning objectives

- To observe and recognize some simple characteristics of animals and plants.
- To know that the group of living things called animals includes humans.

Resources

- "Sorting Plants and Animals" Notebook file
- a selection of images of plants, animals, and inanimate objects for children to sort
- paper
- scissors
- glue
- pencils

Whiteboard tools

- Pen tray
- Select tool
- Highlighter pen

Getting Started

Open the "Sorting Plants and Animals" Notebook file. Ask children to define the words *plant* and *animal*. Record their initial ideas on page 2. Save the Notebook file so that these ideas can be looked at again during Wrap-Up.

Mini-Lesson

1. Read the definitions of *plants* and *animals* on page 3 of the Notebook file and talk about them. Invite a child to come to the SMART Board and use a Highlighter pen to highlight the important words.

2. Show children page 4. Ask them to name the plants, animals, and objects at the bottom of the page.

3. Challenge them to sort the pictures into the three groups—plant, animal, or neither.

4. Begin by finding pictures to add to the animal group. Remind children of the definition of an animal. Guide them to consider humans as part of this group. Show that humans fit the animal definition.

5. If children want to place the teddy bear and rocking horse in the animal box, explain that these things are not alive, and never have been, so they cannot be animals.

6. Next, find pictures to add to the plant group. Remind children of the definition of a plant. Guide them to consider trees for this group. Show that trees fit the plant definition.

7. Check that the remaining pictures should be added to the "neither" group. Help children understand that if the objects are not alive and have never been alive, then they are neither a plant nor an animal and can be added to the "neither" group.

Independent Work

Provide children with sheets of paper and a selection of images to be sorted into three groups: plants, animals, and neither (see Resources). Ask children to divide their pages into three parts and write the appropriate headings at the top of each section. Supply them with scissors and glue and ask them to cut out and stick the pictures into the correct groups. Keep reminding children of the definitions for *plant* and *animal*. Encourage them to check that their sorting choices fit the definitions. Challenge more-confident learners to think of and draw three more things to add to each group.

Wrap-Up

Return to page 2 of the Notebook file (click on the link on page 5). Reread the definitions of *plant* and *animal* that children originally gave. Encourage them to edit the definitions according to what they have learned. Show children some of the pictures that caused discussion during the Independent Work time, and ask them to decide what group they belong to. Always refer back to the definitions to check children's decisions.

Animals and Their Young

Learning objective
- To match young and adults of the same animal.

Resources
- "Animals and Their Young" Notebook file
- "Match the Animals" (p. 62)
- toy animals to represent the images on the reproducible sheet
- nonfiction books showing young and adult of the same animal

Whiteboard tools
- Pen tray
- Select tool
- Delete button

Getting Started

Open page 2 of the "Animals and Their Young" Notebook file and ask children to identify the animals. Ask: *Are there any animals that go together or are similar?* Encourage children to explain their thinking. Use the Delete button (or select the Delete option from the drop-down menu) to remove the large cloud at the top of the page to reveal the question: *Can you match the young and adult of the same animal?* Invite volunteers to come to the SMART Board to move the images to match the young and adult of each animal.

Mini-Lesson

1. Go to page 3 of the Notebook file and read the questions: *How are the adults and young the same? How are the adults and young different?* Ask children to discuss and share ideas with a partner before sharing with the class. Use a pen from the Pen tray to annotate the page with the main points.

2. Repeat the activity on page 4.

Independent Work

Provide each child with a copy of "Match the Animals" (p. 62). Ask children to match the young and adult of each animal by drawing a line to link each pair. Encourage them to name each animal and describe how the animals change as they grow. You may wish to provide nonfiction books showing photographs of young and adult animals, to support children.

Give less-confident learners some toy animals to match, before moving on to matching the images on the reproducible sheet. Focus on the more-obvious pairings before moving on to discuss the less-obvious examples (for example, tadpole/frog, caterpillar/butterfly). Encourage more-confident learners to think of other animals and ask them to draw the young and adult versions.

Wrap-Up

Go to page 5 of the Notebook file and ask for volunteers to match the animals with their young, as they have done for their Independent Work. They can either draw lines or drag and drop the animals. Ask children what they have learned. Share and discuss their work, ensuring that they have matched the young and adult of each animal correctly. Have they learned the names of any new animals and their young? Go to page 6 and ask: *How do animals change as they get older?* It may be easier for children to think about how their own pets, if they have any, have changed. Write their ideas on the page.

Animal Life Cycle

Learning objectives
- To know that animals (including humans) produce young and these grow into children and adults.
- To understand that babies and children need to be looked after while they are growing.
- To ask questions in order to make simple comparisons of babies and children.

Resources
- "Animal Life Cycle" Notebook file
- paper
- pencils

Whiteboard tools
- Pen tray
- Select tool

Before You Start
If possible, before the lesson, invite an adult with a baby to visit the class and talk to children about caring for a baby. (Encourage children to ask sensible questions.)

Getting Started
Explain to children that there are special names for baby animals. Show page 2 of the "Animal Life Cycle" Notebook file. Read the question at the top of the page and encourage children to discuss the answer. Invite a volunteer to press on the animal that they think is the correct answer. If it is correct, they will hear a cheer. Ask children to consider whether the young would look like its mother when it is born and whether it comes from an egg or from its mother's tummy. Repeat for pages 3 to 7.

Mini-Lesson
1. Display pages 8 and 9 of the Notebook file to show the life cycles of a chicken and a frog. Page 10 shows the timeline of a human. First, ask children to explain each life cycle or timeline. Then invite them to drag and drop the pictures into place.

2. Discuss how the animals change from being born to becoming a fully grown adult. Explain that some animals look completely different from their parents when they are young and others, like humans, look very similar.

3. Discuss how long the parents of these different animals care for their young and what needs they have. Compare these needs to the needs of a human infant.

4. Introduce Ellie and Jack on page 11. Relate Jack to the baby that visited the class (see Before You Start), and Ellie to children themselves. Talk briefly about ways in which Ellie and Jack's parents might look after them.

5. Move on to page 12 and consider the questions. Encourage children to answer the questions using the knowledge they gained from the baby visit and what they know about themselves. Write the main points into the boxes.

Independent Work
Fold pieces of paper in half, vertically, and give each child a sheet. Ask children to draw a picture of a baby at the top of the first half and a picture of a child at the top of the second half of the divided page. Beneath the pictures, ask children to record their ideas about the needs of each. Ask: *In what ways do the child and baby need to be looked after? Why is this necessary?*

Supply less-confident learners with prompt questions that they can answer about the needs of babies and children. For example: *What do they eat?* Challenge more-confident learners by asking them to write a paragraph comparing the needs of babies and children (for example, babies only drink milk, but children can eat solid food because they have teeth to chew it).

Wrap-Up
Share some of the children's thoughts from their Independent Work. Address any errors and misconceptions that are evident in their work. Use page 13 to jot down notes. Ask children to explain to a partner two ways in which babies' needs are different from children's needs.

Categorizing Animals

Learning objectives

- To know that living things can be grouped according to observable similarities and differences.
- To present results in a bar graph.

Resources

- "Categorizing Animals" Notebook file
- a selection of images of different animals found in the local area, including humans
- plain paper
- glue
- scissors
- pencils
- graph paper

Whiteboard tools

- Pen tray
- Select tool

Getting Started

Display page 2 of the "Categorizing Animals" Notebook file. Sit children in a circle to play the "Similar and Different" game. Ensure that they know what *similar* and *different* mean. Show pictures of two different animals. Move around the circle, asking children to think of a way that the two animals are either similar or different; the first person has to say a similarity and the second person has to say a difference. When children have run out of ideas, show two more animals.

Mini-Lesson

1. Explain to children that the big group called "animals" can be split up into a number of smaller groups by looking at the similarities between the animals.

2. Give children an example of this by explaining that robins, bees, and butterflies can all be grouped together because they can all fly.

3. Show children page 3 of the Notebook file. Tell them that you have decided to sort the animals into three groups: walk, slither, and fly.

4. Invite individuals to come to the SMART Board and drag and drop the animals into the three different groups.

5. When the animals are sorted, count how many are in each group to see which method of movement is most common. Use page 4 to show how to display children's findings in a bar graph.

6. Show children the pictures that they will be sorting in the Independent Work (see Resources) and ask them to talk to a partner about the different categories they could sort them into.

7. Use page 5 to list the different ideas that children have on how to sort, and leave these on display when children begin their Independent Work.

Independent Work

Divide the class into small groups and give each group a set of pictures to sort. Ask children to decide how they are going to sort the pictures and then draw a chart with the appropriate number of sections on a piece of paper. Make sure that they add a heading to each section. Provide children with glue and scissors. Ask them to cut out and stick the pictures into the appropriate groups. Give children some graph paper or a bar-graph template and ask them to show their results as a bar graph.

Wrap-Up

Invite some children to share their work with the class. Record their responses on page 6 of the Notebook file. Ask children questions about what they found out. Talk with them about some of the terms used to properly classify animals such as *mammal*, *bird*, and *insect*. Work with children to define these categories of animals. Determine which category humans belong to.

What Animals Eat

- To understand that different animals have different diets.
- To raise questions about the diet of different pets.
- To turn ideas about the diet of animals into a form that can be investigated.
- To decide how many animals should be investigated and the range of foods to be considered.
- To present evidence about the foods eaten by animals in a suitable bar graph or pictogram.
- To decide whether the evidence is sufficient to draw conclusions.

Resources
- "What Animals Eat" Notebook file
- "Animal Diets" (p. 63)

Whiteboard tools
- Pen tray
- Select tool
- On-screen Keyboard

(Microsoft Excel is required to view the embedded spreadsheet in the Notebook file.)

Getting Started

Load the "What Animals Eat" Notebook file and go to page 2. Ask children if they own a pet. Take a tally of the type of pets children own using the table on page 2. Create a pictogram or bar graph of the results on page 3. Discuss which pet is the most popular.

Mini-Lesson

1. Ask children about their pets and who is responsible for caring for them, especially for feeding them. Use a pen from the Pen tray to write their responses on page 4 of the Notebook file.

2. Display page 5 and discuss what goldfish eat (don't forget to include naturally occurring pond weed).

3. On page 6, ask children to write on the page the foods that a cat would eat.

4. Tell children that they are going to carry out a survey to find out about the diet of an animal. Emphasize that *diet* means what an animal eats (not a weight-loss program).

5. Go to page 7. Decide upon a question to investigate (such as: *Do all dogs eat the same food?*) Write this at the top of the page.

6. Discuss how many animals you are going to try to survey (pets at home, neighbors' pets, and so on) and choose six sorts of food (such as fish, chicken, dried food, and so on).

7. Hand out copies of "Animal Diets" (p. 63) and ask children to fill in the names of the six sorts of food in the first column.

Independent Work

Ask children to complete the sheet for homework. Ask parents or guardians to supervise their children when asking neighbors for the information or when telephoning friends and relatives. Ensure that children only tick the right column of the sheet if the animal in question has ever eaten that sort of food, not if the animal probably would. Extend the activity by asking children to predict the overall outcome of the survey.

Wrap-Up

Ask a number of children to present the results of their own surveys. Inform children that bar graphs can be used to present results clearly so that comparisons can be made more easily. Go to page 8 and open the "Animal diets investigation" spreadsheet to input children's results. Tally the results for each sort of food and use the On-screen Keyboard to enter the data into the spreadsheet cells on the worksheet. Examine and discuss the resulting bar graph. Ask children what they can conclude (for example, half of the dogs eat beef). Consider how accurate the survey was. Discuss whether there is enough evidence to draw accurate conclusions (relatively few animals were surveyed and dogs might eat other sorts of food if they were given the opportunity). Write these points on page 8.

Different Materials

Learning objectives
- To know that every material has many properties that can be recognized using our senses, and described using appropriate vocabulary.
- To record observations of materials.

Resources
- "Different Materials" Notebook file
- "Identifying and Describing Materials" (p. 64)
- a variety of objects made from different materials, including wood, metal, plastic, fabric, sand, and glass (such as bottle, glove, spoon, and so on)

Whiteboard tools
- Pen tray
- Select tool
- Delete button

Getting Started

Display page 2 of the "Different Materials" Notebook file. Ask children to identify some of the objects on the page. Allow them to handle the real objects made from a variety of materials, asking and answering the questions on the page.

Go to page 3 and ask children to name the types of materials the different objects were made from: wood, metal, plastic, fabric, sand, and glass. Write these on the Notebook page. Ask children to identify further examples of each material in the classroom.

Mini-Lesson

1. Go to page 4 of the Notebook file and read the questions. Using some of the objects from Getting Started, ask children to provide answers to the two questions. Write a list of suggested descriptive words on the Notebook page.

2. Move to page 5. Using the list of common materials on page 3 and the descriptive words on page 4, ask children to help you complete the sentences: *This is a ___ (bottle). It is made from ___ (glass). It is ___* (transparent, smooth, and breakable). You may want to have a real bottle available for children to examine.

3. Use pages 6 and 7 for further reinforcement of the descriptive activity. Page 6 shows an image of a glove, and page 7 shows an image of a spoon. Again, it would be helpful if you could provide a real example of each item for children to look at and hold.

Independent Work

Hand out copies of "Identifying and Describing Materials" (p. 64) and provide a range of objects made from different materials. Ask children to choose three different objects and complete the sentences on the sheet for each object: *This is a ___. It is made from ___. It is ___* (descriptive words). You may wish to display the materials words and the descriptive words provided by children during the Mini-Lesson, to support children in their writing.

Give less-confident learners a word bank to draw from for their descriptive phrases. Encourage them to spend time looking at each object, and then to hold it and shut their eyes so that they can concentrate on what the object feels like. Encourage more-confident learners to think of additional new words to describe the objects.

Wrap-Up

Open page 8 of the Notebook file. Read the descriptions of each object and ask children to predict which kitchen object is hidden under the blue box (you may wish to have real examples or pictures of the items available for them to choose from). Select the box under each description and press the Delete button (or select the Delete option from the drop-down menu) to reveal the object. Repeat the activity on pages 9 and 10. Go to page 11 and ask children what they have found out or learned from their explorations. Make notes on the Notebook page.

Grouping Materials

Learning objective
- To know that there are many materials and these can be named and described.

Resources
- "Grouping Materials" Notebook file
- a range of objects made from wood, metal, plastic, fabric, and glass

Whiteboard tools
- Pen tray
- Select tool

Getting Started

Remind children of previous work on identifying and describing materials. Go to page 2 of the "Grouping Materials" Notebook file and ask them to recall the names of the common materials objects are made from: wood, metal, glass, fabric, and plastic. Write their answers on the Notebook page. Ask children to describe each material and give examples of objects made from it. Go to page 3 and ask children to sort the objects on the page according to the material they are made from.

Mini-Lesson

1. Display page 4 of the Notebook file and ask children to identify objects in the kitchen that are made from wood, plastic, metal, glass, and fabric. Ask for volunteers to circle the object in the same color as the "material" word at the bottom of the page.

2. Ask children to suggest other items that could be added to the Notebook file that would be made from each of the materials. Allow them to draw their suggestions on the page.

Independent Work

Ask children to work in pairs to explore the classroom and find objects made from each of the common materials—wood, metal, plastic, fabric, and glass. Invite them to record their findings either in the form of a simple table, by drawing the objects and adding labels, or by sticking prepared written labels on the items found within the classroom. You may want to set up some tables with a range of objects made from different materials for children to sort into groups. Encourage children to describe the properties of the materials as they explore and sort.

Pair less-confident learners with a more-confident partner to help guide their exploration and discussion. Challenge more-confident learners to add some words to describe each material, using terms such as *hard, bendy, shiny*, and so on.

Wrap-Up

Invite children to share the objects they found that were made from each material. Go to page 5 of the Notebook file and ask children to discuss why different objects are made from different materials. Use examples from the Independent Work. For example: *Why are some sinks made from metal? Why are pencils made from wood?* Go to page 6 and ask children what they have learned today. Note down their responses on the Notebook page.

Natural vs. Manmade

Learning objectives
- To know that some materials occur naturally and some do not.
- To know the names of some naturally occurring materials.
- To know that some naturally occurring materials are treated before they are used.

Resources
- "Natural vs. Manmade" Notebook file
- a variety of objects made from natural and manmade materials
- glue
- scissors
- individual whiteboards and pens

Whiteboard tools
- Pen tray
- Select tool

Getting Started
Provide children with a variety of different objects and ask them to sort the objects according to the material they are made from. Encourage children to add labels to each of their groups. Look at some of the objects and talk about the characteristics of the material from which they are made. Review some of the vocabulary they have learned for describing materials, such as *transparent*, *rough*, and so on. Record key words on page 2 of the "Natural vs. Manmade" Notebook file.

Mini-Lesson
1. Introduce the terms *natural material* and *manmade material*. Explain that a natural material is not produced by humans—it is a material that is made from a plant or an animal, or is found under the ground. Ask children to think of some examples of natural materials, such as wood and wool.
2. Use page 3 of the Notebook file to sort materials into natural and manmade. Ensure that children understand these terms properly.
3. Explain the difference between *manufactured* and *not manufactured*. Make sure that children understand that natural materials can be manufactured into useful objects (such as paper or a knitted sweater) but that the material the object is made from is still natural.
4. Explain that a manmade material would not exist if man didn't make it using chemicals in a factory (such as plastic or nylon).
5. Go to page 4 and encourage children to talk to a partner about how to sort the objects using the table. Support their decision-making process with appropriate questioning.

Independent Work
Provide a wide selection of natural and manmade materials that are suitable for use in a collage. Put children into groups of three. Ask each group to choose whether they want to create a collage made from natural materials or from manmade materials. Give the groups a theme for their collage, such as fairy-tale characters. Challenge them to create it using the material type of their choice. Ensure that the groups are of mixed ability so that the less-confident learners are supported in their decision making. Encourage children to talk about the origins and properties of the materials they are using as they work.

Wrap-Up
Show each collage to the class and ask them to guess whether the group chose to use manmade or natural materials for their collage. Challenge children to find any materials from the wrong group that have mistakenly been included in the collages. As a final assessment, ask children to list on their individual whiteboards five objects in the classroom that are made from natural materials and five that are made from manmade materials. Beside the object name, ask children to write the name of the material that the object is made from. This can be modeled on page 5 of the Notebook file.

Squashing, Bending, Twisting, Stretching

Learning objectives

- To know that objects made from some materials can be altered by squashing, bending, twisting, and stretching.
- To describe ways of making materials or objects change, using appropriate vocabulary.
- To explore materials using appropriate senses and make observations and simple comparisons.
- To construct a table to record observations.

Resources

- "Squashing, Bending, Twisting, Stretching" Notebook file
- "Twist and Stretch!" (p. 65)
- play dough
- elastic bands
- pebbles
- clay
- foam balls

Whiteboard tools

- Pen tray
- Select tool

Getting Started

Open the "Squashing, Bending, Twisting, Stretching" Notebook file and go to page 2. Ask children to work with a partner to think of different ways that a material, such as play dough, can be changed. Listen to the ideas as a class. Encourage children to consider whether all materials can be changed in the same ways. For example, can all materials be stretched?

Mini-Lesson

1. Go to page 3 of the Notebook file. Give each child a piece of play dough and ask children to squash it. Show them what squashing means with your own piece of play dough.

2. Next ask children to bend, twist, and stretch the play dough. Ensure that all of the children understand this vocabulary.

3. Show children some play dough, an elastic band, a pebble, some clay, and a foam ball. Talk about the properties of each object in turn.

4. Now show children the table on page 4 of the Notebook file. Ask them to predict whether each of the materials will squash, bend, twist, or stretch. Allow them to record their predictions with a tick or cross in the appropriate box.

5. Encourage children to predict whether the object will return to its original state once a force is no longer being applied to it, or whether it will remain distorted like the play dough does.

Independent Work

Supply children with a copy of "Twist and Stretch!" (p. 65) and the five materials to be tested—play dough, an elastic band, a pebble, some clay, and a foam ball. Ask children to test the materials and complete the table with their actual results. Challenge more-confident learners to create their own table to record their results. Talk to children about whether or not the results were as they expected.

Wrap-Up

Gather children together and use page 5 of the Notebook file to record the results of their experiments. Discuss the results with children and talk about anything that surprised them. Make a note of interesting observations or comments on page 6. Ask some questions about the materials, such as: *Can you keep stretching an elastic band? Once an elastic band has snapped, will it still return to its original state? Is there any way that you could change a pebble? Can anything be squashed but not stretched?* Discuss children's answers to these questions.

Heating Materials

Learning objectives

- To know that materials often change when they are heated.
- To make observations and simple comparisons.
- To use a table to make a record of observations.
- To decide whether or not what happened was what they expected.

Resources

- "Heating Materials" Notebook file
- "Putting on the Heat" (p. 66)
- four different types of candies (for example, chocolate, caramel, chewing gum, hard candy)
- cupcake or other baked good
- slice of bread
- paper towels

Safety note: Check for any food allergies before children eat or handle the foods.

Whiteboard tools

- Pen tray
- Select tool

Getting Started

Open the "Heating Materials" Notebook file and go to page 2. Show children a cupcake and ask them if it has always looked like it does now. Encourage them to think about how the cupcake turned from a bowl of mixed ingredients into a cupcake. Establish that the ingredients changed as they were heated. Ask children to consider whether or not the cupcake could be turned back into its original separate ingredients.

Mini-Lesson

1. Show children a slice of bread and ask them to describe to a partner what will happen to it as it is heated.

2. Display the photographs on page 3 of the Notebook file. Challenge children to place the photographs in order, according to the amount that the bread has been heated.

3. Ask them to think about whether the toast will return to its original state when it is cooled.

4. Invite children to think of other things that change when they are heated. Can they think of any materials other than food? Ask them to consider whether the materials will return to their original state once they have cooled.

Independent Work

Tell children that they are going to find out what happens to different candies as they are heated. Explain that they are going to use the heat from their hands to heat the candies, as it is safer than using a candle.

Start off by asking children to wash their hands. Supply paper towels to wipe their hands during the experiment. Give each child a copy of "Putting on the Heat" (p. 66). Show them the four candies they will be investigating. Ask them to make detailed predictions about what will happen to each candy as it is heated in their hands. Tell children to hold the first candy in a closed hand and then use the on-screen timer on page 4 of the Notebook file to time three minutes. Invite children to open their hands, describe what has happened to the candy, and record their observations in the table. Repeat this cycle until all of the candies have been tested. As an extra challenge, ask children to complete the bottom section of the reproducible sheet.

Wrap-Up

Add the names of the candies to the table on page 5 of the Notebook file. Compile the results of the experiment as a class. Find out whether children were surprised by any of the results or whether they made accurate predictions. Address any misconceptions that may arise during the discussion. Use page 6 for notes. Ask children to consider what would have happened if the candies had been heated with a candle instead. Invite them to decide what would have happened to each candy if it had been left to cool.

Properties of Materials

Learning objectives

- To identify a range of common materials and know that the same material is used to make different objects.
- To recognize properties such as hardness, strength, and flexibility, and compare materials in terms of these properties.

Resources

- "Properties of Materials" Notebook file
- "What Are the Properties?" (p. 67)
- objects made from a range of materials, including metal, wood, rubber, plastic, rock, leather, wool, cotton, glass, and ceramics
- magnifying glasses

Whiteboard tools

- Pen tray
- Select tool

Getting Started

Ask children to do a quick survey of the classroom (or another safe location) to identify a range of materials. Discuss why particular materials might have been used (for example, metal for chair legs, wood for floors). Use a pen from the Pen tray to write their ideas on page 2 of the "Properties of Materials" Notebook file.

Mini-Lesson

1. Display page 3 of the Notebook file and discuss the errors in the labeling of the objects. Establish the difference between the name of an object and the name of the material it is made from.

2. Invite individual children to drag and drop the objects to match the correct labels.

3. Challenge children to think of other objects made from the materials listed.

4. Use page 4 of the Notebook file to challenge children to think about what material an object is made from and identify objects that are made from the same material. Have children drag and drop the objects in the box into groups, under the appropriate labels, on the SMART Board.

5. Discuss any misconceptions and surprises. Guide children to conclude that the same material can be used to make different objects and that some objects are made from more than one material (such as the well or the mirror).

Independent Work

Hand out a copy of "What Are the Properties?" (p. 67) to each child. Ask children to observe carefully and feel a number of different objects. In each case, ask children to sketch the object, identify the material that it is made from, and record its properties (for example, smooth, flexible, transparent, hard).

Help less-confident learners to choose and record appropriate properties from the word bank on the sheet. Challenge more-confident learners by asking them to compare materials in terms of their properties (for example, ask: *Which materials seem to be the strongest or most flexible?*)

Wrap-Up

Ask children to take turns describing an object. Invite each child to describe the object using only the properties of the material from which it is made. Can the other children identify the object being described? With children's help, write the properties of each material in the space on page 5. Discuss which materials have common properties and which differ. Challenge children to think about why particular properties are better suited to the function of an object (for example, although both plastic and glass are transparent, a ruler is made from plastic because it is more flexible and less fragile).

Investigation: Absorbency

Learning objectives
- To plan a test to compare the absorbency of different papers, deciding what evidence to collect, considering what to change, what to keep the same, and what to measure.
- To make comparisons and draw conclusions.

Resources
- "Investigation: Absorbency" Notebook file
- a range of different paper towels (up to five brands)
- scissors
- rulers
- water
- food coloring
- measuring cups, pipettes, or syringes
- clear plastic cups

Whiteboard tools
- Pen tray
- Select tool
- Screen Shade

Getting Started
Ask children if they have ever spilled any liquid at home, particularly in the kitchen, and how these spills are usually cleared up. Find out what they know about relevant household cleaning products and how they are advertised.

Mini-Lesson
1. Display the ad for a paper towel on page 2 of the "Investigation: Absorbency" Notebook file. Discuss the key features of the ad and how realistic its claims seem.

2. Discuss how children could go about finding the best kitchen towel. Establish what *best* would mean and how this could be translated into an investigation, including the resources they would need and how they could make the test fair.

3. Go to page 3 and fill in the criteria for a fair and accurate investigation into the three labeled boxes. You could use the Screen Shade to cover the word bank at the bottom of the screen in advance to challenge children to think of the correct vocabulary. Write in the relevant boxes what they are going to keep the same (the size of the towel/amount of water), what they will change (the type of towel), and what they will measure (how much towel is needed).

4. Uncover the word bank and, together, drag and drop relevant phrases into the appropriate boxes.

Independent Work
Ask children to cut up some small, equally sized pieces of each of the different brands of paper towel. Using an equal quantity of water in a cup each time, ask children to count how many pieces of each type of towel are required to soak up all the water. You may wish to use food coloring to increase the visibility of the liquid. Help children record their results in a simple table.

Support less-confident learners by discussing how the fair testing will help produce more accurate results. Challenge more-confident learners by asking them to establish some reasons as to why a certain towel performs better than another and to predict how the next towel will perform based on such reasons.

Wrap-Up
Try to establish a consensus in ranking the towels in order of absorbency, completing the results table on page 4 of the Notebook file. You will need to collect all the answers and then address any differences first. Discuss how multiple results help to establish a consensus (or highlight inconsistencies) and draw out children's ideas about why certain towels are more absorbent than others.

Investigation: Stretchiness

Learning objectives

- To plan how to find out which pair of tights is stretchiest, making a fair comparison.
- To decide what to change, what to keep the same, and what to measure.
- To make careful measurements of length, to present measurements as a bar graph, and to draw conclusions.

Resources

- "Investigation: Stretchiness" Notebook file
- "Stretching Investigation" (p. 68)
- a maximum of six pairs of tights of the same size but different thicknesses (cut the legs to the same length)
- sets of weights
- meter sticks, rulers, or tape measures

Whiteboard tools

- Pen tray
- Select tool
- Screen Shade
- On-screen Keyboard

(Microsoft Excel is required to view the embedded spreadsheet.)

Getting Started

Ask children to examine some pairs of tights and describe some of their properties, including any differences in thickness and stretchiness. Consider together why tights are designed in different thicknesses. Ask children whether they think thickness affects how stretchy the tights are. Write their responses on page 2 of the "Investigation: Stretchiness" Notebook file.

Mini-Lesson

1. Discuss how children could go about finding out which pair of tights is the stretchiest. Establish how this could be transformed into an investigation, including the resources they would need and how they could ensure a fair test.

2. Go to page 3. If required, cover the word bank at the bottom of the screen in advance by using the Screen Shade. Challenge children to think of what they are going to keep the same in the investigation (weight), what they will change (the thickness of tights), and what they will measure (how far the tights stretch).

3. Reveal the word bank, and drag and drop relevant phrases into the correct boxes.

Independent Work

Hand out copies of "Stretching Investigation" (p. 68) to each child. Ask children to predict which tights will be the most or least stretchy (or in-between), adding *most stretchy* and *least stretchy* for the appropriate tights in the "My prediction" column. Ask children to secure a set weight to, or in, each pair of tights and carefully measure the length of the stretched tights. Remind them to keep their feet out of the way or to place a box or bin underneath the suspended weight. Ask children to record their measurements accurately on their sheets.

Support less-confident learners by ensuring that each measurement is made and recorded accurately. Challenge more-confident learners by asking them to predict how stretchy each pair of tights will be before measuring.

Wrap-Up

Discuss what children discovered. Inform children that bar graphs can be used to present results clearly so that comparisons can be made more easily. Press the hyperlinked button on page 4 of the Notebook page to open the "Stretching Investigations" spreadsheet. Use the On-screen Keyboard to enter children's data in the table. The bar graph will fill in automatically. Examine and discuss the resulting bar graph, using it to explain which tights were stretchiest. Establish if there is any link between thickness and stretchiness. Use page 5 to make notes on what children learned.

Pushing and Pulling

Learning objectives

- To understand that pushing or pulling things can make objects start or stop moving.
- To identify similarities and differences between the movement of different objects.
- To make suggestions about how objects can be made to move and to find out whether or not the ideas worked.

Resources

- "Pushing and Pulling" Notebook file
- "Pushes and Pulls Around the House" (p. 69)
- objects for modeling push and pull actions (for example, zipper, roll of toilet paper, cell phone, toaster, light switch, and so on)
- objects that are moved or operated with a push or pull action
- sticky notes or labels with the words *push* and *pull* written on them

Whiteboard tools

- Pen tray
- Select tool

Getting Started

Review any previous explorations of different types of movement. Ask children how the toys pictured on page 2 of the "Pushing and Pulling" Notebook file could be moved. Have them demonstrate the actions and give reasons for their suggestions. Write the correct answers (*push* or *pull*) beneath each picture, ensuring that children understand and know the difference between the two forces.

Mini-Lesson

1. Go to page 3 of the Notebook file and read the question: *What other things do we push or pull?* Ask children to discuss and share ideas with a partner. Write or draw their ideas on the page, encouraging them to demonstrate the force (push or pull) being used—where possible, with a real object.

2. Go to page 4. Ask children to drag the pictures out of the box at the bottom of the page and sort them into either push or pull actions.

3. Model the force used on the different objects if you have any real versions of the items available.

Independent Work

Hand out *push* and *pull* sticky notes or labels. Ask children, in pairs, to explore the classroom and place the *push* or *pull* labels on items that are moved or operated with either force. Encourage children to discuss their actions when making the objects move or operate. You may want to set up a table with some specific objects for them to explore.

Less-confident learners should work with more-confident partners. Encourage them to experience the pushing and pulling for themselves, so that they understand the difference between the two forces. Encourage more-confident learners to find objects that are moved or operated by both a push and a pull action.

Wrap-Up

Go to page 5 of the Notebook file. Ask children what they have found or learned from their exploration. Share findings for objects that were moved or operated by a pushing action and then for objects that were moved or operated by a pulling action. Ask: *Were there any objects that moved or operated by both a push and a pull?* Explain how the Venn diagram can be used to show children's findings. Record a range of their findings using the Venn diagram on page 5. Hand out copies of "Pushes and Pulls Around the House" (p. 69) and explain to children how to complete it for homework.

What Makes It Move?

Learning objectives

- To understand that it is not only ourselves that make things move by pushing.
- To ask questions about what is causing movement.

Resources

- "What Makes It Move?" Notebook file
- toy boat in a large container of water
- straws for blowing
- a range of toys that are moved by wind or water (for example, toy windmill, bubbles, blow football, kite, sailboat)

Whiteboard tools

- Pen tray
- Select tool

Getting Started

Open page 2 of the "What Makes It Move?" Notebook file. Read the question: *How can things be moved?* Remind children of previous work on exploring things that moved by being pushed or pulled (see p. 35) and write down some of these things. Point out that all these things are pushed or pulled by a person. Ask: *Can you think of anything else that might make something move?*

Go to page 3. Ask: *How could we make this boat move without touching it?* If possible, present this scenario with a toy boat in a large container of water. Write children's suggestions on the page. Ask volunteers to demonstrate and to identify the cause of motion (for example, blowing into the sails or making waves in the water to move it).

Mini-Lesson

1. Go to page 4 of the Notebook file. Ask children to identify what could be moving in the picture and to suggest what could be causing the movement. Make a note of their suggestions.

2. Repeat the above activity with the images on pages 5 to 8.

3. Establish with children that it is not only people that make things move by pushing; wind and water can also make things move.

Independent Work

Give children a range of toys that are moved by wind or water. Ask them to explore how each toy moves, to describe the movement, and to identify what causes it to move. Encourage them to ask one another questions about what is causing the movement.

Less-confident learners could be paired with more-confident partners to facilitate discussion or grouped together to work with the teacher or teaching assistant to guide their exploration. Encourage more-confident learners to think about whether the wind and water are pushing or pulling the object. Ask children to sort the toys into two categories: those that are moved by wind and those that are moved by water.

Wrap-Up

Discuss how children sorted the toys, and compare results. Emphasize that these toys are not being pushed or pulled by a person. Go to page 9 of the Notebook file and ask children if they can think of any other things that are made to move by the wind or by water. Go to page 10. Ask children what they have learned during the lesson, and record their conclusions on the Notebook page.

Types of Vehicles and Speed

Learning objectives

- To consider the ways in which different objects move.
- To make measurements of distance and record these in a prepared table.
- To use the results in a table to draw a bar graph.
- To decide whether a comparison was fair.

Resources

- "Types of Vehicles and Speed" Notebook file
- "Vehicle Test" (p. 70)
- a range of toy vehicles
- measuring tools

Whiteboard tools

- Pen tray
- Select tool
- On-screen Keyboard

(Microsoft Excel is required to view the embedded spreadsheet in the Notebook file.)

Getting Started

Display page 2 of the "Types of Vehicles and Speed" Notebook file. Show children five toy vehicles (see Resources) and ask them to explain how they could make the vehicles move (by pushing them) and how they could make them move faster (by pushing harder). Ask children to consider if there are any other factors that could affect the speed at which the vehicles move.

Mini-Lesson

1. Examine the five toy vehicles closely. Talk about their properties (the heaviest, longest, one with the biggest wheels, and so on). Make a note of key words on page 3 of the Notebook file.

2. Ask children to predict which of the vehicles will travel the farthest and have them explain why they think so. Write their predictions into the table on page 4.

3. Open the spreadsheet by pressing the link on page 4 of the Notebook file. Draw a starting line on a smooth flat surface. Push the vehicles, one at a time, with an equal force from the starting line.

4. Support children as they measure the distance each vehicle travels and record these results in the top table in the spreadsheet (Test 1). Use the On-screen Keyboard to enter data on the spreadsheet. A bar graph of the data should appear next to the table.

5. Look at the results with children and encourage them to evaluate whether or not their predictions were correct. Invite them to suggest reasons why the results are as they are.

6. Repeat the same experiment, but this time, allow a different child to push each vehicle from the starting line.

7. Record the results in the bottom table (Test 2) and compare the two sets of results.

8. Ask children to consider why the results might be different. Ask: *Was the test a fair test? How could we make the test fair?* Conclude that the same person needs to push each vehicle with the same force to make the test fair.

Independent Work

Partner up children and supply each pair with five toy vehicles. Ask them to predict which one will travel the farthest and why. Support the pairs in independently carrying out the experiment from the Mini-Lesson. Ensure that children consider whether or not the test is a fair test. Give each pair a copy of "Vehicle Test" (p. 70). Ask them to record the distance each vehicle traveled. Ask children to create a bar graph using the measurements collected and then evaluate their initial predictions.

Wrap-Up

Invite children to talk about their investigations. Ask: *Did any of the results surprise you? Why do you think this vehicle traveled farthest? How did you make the test fair?* Return to the Notebook file and record children's responses on page 5 of the Notebook file.

Ramp Height and Speed

Learning objectives

- To suggest an experiment to test and predict what will happen.
- To decide what to do and what measurements to take.
- To make measurements and record these in a prepared table.
- To use the results in a table to draw a bar graph.
- To say whether the prediction was correct and try to explain the results.

Resources

- "Ramp Height and Speed" Notebook file
- "Ramp Height" (p. 71)
- ramps and blocks
- rulers
- toy cars
- measuring tools

Whiteboard tools

- Pen tray
- Select tool
- On-screen Keyboard

(Microsoft Excel is required to view the embedded spreadsheet in the Notebook file.)

Getting Started

Show children how to build a ramp. Ask them to roll some different vehicles down the ramp and discuss how they traveled. Ask: *How could you make the vehicle move faster or slower?* Elicit that altering the ramp height could change the speed of the vehicle. Go to page 2 of the "Ramp Height and Speed" Notebook file to model how a ramp can be built. Select the blue ramp, then press and drag the right-hand white circle to adjust the ramp height.

Mini-Lesson

1. Show children a low ramp and a high ramp. Ask them to predict which ramp would make a vehicle travel fastest and to explain why they think this. Record their predictions on page 3 of the Notebook file.

2. Explain that if a vehicle travels faster it will also travel farther before it stops. Suggest that measuring the distance a vehicle traveled from the end of the ramp will indicate how fast it was traveling.

3. Ask: *What factors do we need to consider to make the test fair? Would it be fair to use a different vehicle each time?*

4. Open the spreadsheet by pressing the link on page 3. Draw a starting line on the ramp and raise it with one block. Release the vehicle from behind the starting line without pushing it.

5. Support children as they measure the distance the vehicle travels from the bottom of the ramp. Show them how to use the On-screen Keyboard to record the measurement in the table.

6. Repeat this with the ramp raised up two, three, four, and five blocks.

7. Look at the results with children and encourage them to evaluate whether or not their predictions were correct. Can they suggest reasons for why they got the results they did?

Independent Work

Partner up children and supply each pair with a ramp, five blocks, a ruler, and a toy vehicle. Ask them to carry out the experiment from the Mini-Lesson independently to see if they get the same results. Reinforce that repeating a test makes results more trustworthy. Ensure that children consider whether the test they are carrying out is a fair test. Give each pair a copy of "Ramp Height" (p. 71). Tell them to use this sheet to record the distance that each ramp height makes the vehicle travel. Ask children to create a bar graph using the measurements collected, and then evaluate their initial predictions.

Wrap-Up

Compare children's results with the results found in the Mini-Lesson. Work with children to suggest reasons for any discrepancies if they arise. Display page 4 of the Notebook file and invite one pair to enter their information on the bar graph. They will need to label the axes. Ask children to try to explain the reasons for their results to a partner.

Sources of Light

Learning objectives
- To know that there are many sources of light.
- To know that sources of light vary in brightness.
- To observe and make comparisons of sources of light.

Resources
- "Sources of Light" Notebook file
- "Light Sources Around the House" (p. 72)
- story or poem about darkness and light (for example, *Can't You Sleep, Little Bear?* or *The Owl Who Was Afraid of the Dark*)
- flashlight, candle in a lantern, lamp, metal spoon, silver coin, foil or shiny paper, mirror
- shopping catalogs
- large sheets of paper

Whiteboard tools
- Pen tray
- Select tool
- Spotlight tool

Getting Started

Open page 2 of the "Sources of Light" Notebook file and ask children what they know about the word *light*. Write their responses on the page. Display page 3 and ask them to identify objects within the classroom that are sources of light. Make a note of their suggestions. Discuss the different light sources with regard to whether the object gives out light, reflects it, or lets light pass through it. Enable the Spotlight tool and go to page 4. Use the spotlight to find light sources in the pictured classroom. Are any of these light sources in children's own classroom?

Mini-Lesson

1. Read a story or poem about darkness and light (see Resources). Ask children to identify the light sources in the story or poem.

2. Display page 5 of the Notebook file and ask the class which objects on the page would make good light sources. Where relevant, link this activity to the poem or story. For example: *Which of these objects could have been used to light up the dark in Little Bear's cave?* Drag the objects that children predict to be light sources (or not light sources) into the relevant columns.

3. Test the predictions in a dark place or room. Ensure that children can distinguish between objects that give out light and objects that reflect light. They should check their findings with the predictions they made. Discuss any misunderstandings.

Independent Work

Take children on a "light source" hunt around the school—for example, ceiling lights, computer monitor lights, and motion detector lights. Ask them to draw and label as many light sources as they can. Using shop catalogs, cut out pictures of objects that would give out light (such as televisions, lamps, microwave ovens, and so on). Have children work in groups to create collages of light sources using the ideas and images from the above activities and drawings of their own.

Group less-confident learners with more-confident learners for the collage activity. If the concept needs reinforcement, provide them with some pictures of objects that do and do not give out light to sort into groups. Encourage more-confident learners to think of objects that would not be found within the school or inside the catalogs, and make drawings of these—for example, illuminated shop signs, the moon, or car headlights.

Wrap-Up

Ask children to show their light-source collages. Encourage them to compare the light sources in terms of brightness. Display page 6 of the Notebook file and ask children what they have learned today. Provide each child with a copy of "Light Sources Around the House" (p. 72). Discuss the sheet, explaining to children how to complete it, and give it as homework.

How Shadows Form

- To know that shadows are formed when light traveling from a source is blocked.
- To make and record observations and to present information in drawing and writing.

Resources
- "How Shadows Form" Notebook file
- "Shadow Investigations" (p. 73)
- a selection of opaque objects, such as a comb or toy car
- a cardboard tube
- flashlights or other more powerful light sources, such as an overhead projector
- large sheets of white card

Whiteboard tools
- Pen tray
- Select tool
- Pen tool
- Lines tool

Getting Started

Ask children to identify any dark shadows around the classroom and to explain why the shadows are there. Discuss and write their responses on page 2 of the "How Shadows Form" Notebook file. For a more dramatic demonstration, stand or hold an object in front of the beam from the projector, and ask children to discuss what they can and cannot see on the whiteboard. Take care to avoid looking directly into the projector beam.

Mini-Lesson

1. Display page 3 of the Notebook file and discuss what is missing from the picture (a shadow on the board).

2. Ask children to draw a black shadow onto the correct place by either drawing an outline or cloning the hand on the page, and using the Pen tool to fill it with black.

3. Ask children to explain what happens to the light from the projector on its way to the board. Invite individual children to represent their ideas by drawing on screen. Do not, at this stage, inform children that they must draw straight lines to represent light (as children often think light bends around an object).

4. Discuss children's ideas. Next, display and discuss page 4. Establish that light travels in straight lines and a shadow is formed when light is blocked by an object.

5. Discuss any misconceptions and surprises. For example, shine a flashlight directly through a cardboard tube and then twist the tube to one side to demonstrate that light does not bend around corners.

Independent Work

Hand out a copy of the "Shadow Investigations" sheet (p. 73) to each child. Ask children to explore and observe shadow formation by using flashlights or other light sources and an opaque object to form shadows on white card. Tell children to carefully record one of their observations (in drawing and writing) on the reproducible sheet as directed. Extend the activity by asking children to explain why a shadow is larger when an object is closer to the light source.

Wrap-Up

Discuss children's observations. Use page 5 of the Notebook file to test children's learning by inviting them to drag and drop the correct words into each sentence. Emphasize that light travels from a source, not from the eyes.

Investigation: Shadow Length

Learning objectives

- To know that shadows change in length and position throughout the day.
- To measure the length of a shadow in standard measures.
- To make a table and line graph to show how the length of shadows changes during the day.

Resources

- "Investigation: Shadow Length" Notebook file
- "Investigation Planning" (p. 74)
- a long "shadow" stick and base, such as a tee-ball set
- a meter stick showing cm
- chalk or masking tape
- a digital camera (optional)
- a sunny day!

Whiteboard tools

- Pen tray
- Select tool
- On-screen Keyboard

(Microsoft Excel is required to view the embedded spreadsheet in the Notebook file.)

Getting Started

Go to page 2 of the "Investigation: Shadow Length" Notebook file. Ask children if they have noticed differences in the size of shadows at different times of day. (Some children may have noticed long shadows at sunset or short ones at noon in midsummer.) Ask them why shadows might change size during the day. Tell children that they are going to investigate exactly how the length of a shadow changes during a day at school.

Mini-Lesson

1. Ask children how they would plan an investigation to find out how the length of a shadow changes over five or six hours. They also need to think about the resources they would need. Make notes on page 3 of the Notebook file.

2. Discuss how children could make the test fair by asking them what they are going to keep the same (size and position of stick), what they will change (position of the sun in sky), and what they will measure (length of shadow). Drag and drop the correct phrases into the relevant boxes on page 4 of the Notebook file together.

3. Demonstrate how to measure distances of under and over one meter accurately in centimeters, using a meter stick.

4. Ask children to complete their own copies of the "Investigation Planning" reproducible sheet (p. 74). Have them draw and label the setup.

5. Display page 5 and encourage children to predict what will happen.

Independent Work

Set up the "shadow" stick in a flat location that will remain undisturbed and in direct sunlight for the day. At half-hourly intervals, ask children to mark the current shadow using chalk or tape and to measure and record its length and the time accurately. If possible, record this with a digital camera as well. Provide support where necessary.

Wrap-Up

Discuss the pattern made by the different length markings around the shadow stick, asking children what they think has happened. Inform children that a line graph can be used to show how shadow length changes over time. Press the hyperlinked button on page 6 of the Notebook file to open a spreadsheet to record children's results. Use the On-screen Keyboard to enter their data into the table. Discuss the resulting line graph, explaining how the shadow shortens toward noon and lengthens into the afternoon. Compare the results with the predictions. Ask children to explain why the shadow changes length in this way (shadows shorten in the morning as the sun rises higher in the sky and lengthen in the afternoons as the sun sets). Encourage children to explain the movement of the shadow around the stick (the sun moves across the sky from east to west, so light and shadows are cast from different directions). Use page 7 to demonstrate this and display children's photos of the stick and shadow, if available. Repeat this investigation in a different season and compare the results (shadow length in winter will be longer than in summer as the sun travels lower across the sky due to the Earth's tilt and orbit around the sun).

Using Shadows to Tell Time

Learning objective
- To know that shadows can be used to tell the approximate time of day.

Resources
- "Using Shadows to Tell Time" Notebook file
- "Make Your Own Sundial" (p. 75), photocopied onto cardstock, if possible
- magnetic compass
- scissors
- sticky tape or masking tape
- a sunny day!

Whiteboard tools
- Pen tray
- Select tool

Getting Started
At the beginning of the day, ask any children with watches to remove them. If possible, remove or cover the classroom clock. Before the lesson starts, ask children to estimate the time, justifying their estimates.

Inform them that digital watches were invented less than 50 years ago and mechanical watches appeared about 500 years ago, yet the Ancient Egyptians had ways of telling the time nearly 5,000 years ago. How do children think people would have told the time before clocks and watches?

Mini-Lesson
1. Discuss how each object on pages 2 to 5 of the "Using Shadows to Tell Time" Notebook file could have been used to tell the time.

2. Ask children to circle the objects that rely on light and shadows (the Egyptian obelisk and sundial) and label them.

3. Discuss children's familiarity with sundials and display page 6, explaining that the dial's shadow is used to tell the time. Point out that the *gnomon* is the part of the sundial that projects the shadow, which is used to tell the time.

4. Encourage them to say how the dial works, using the phrases on the page to guide them.

5. Tell children that they are going to make their own simple sundials, and display page 7.

6. Drag the gnomon over the base to demonstrate where it fits. Use the right-angled corner to emphasize the correct orientation of the gnomon.

7. Display page 8. Tell children that they will be using a magnetic compass to make sure that their sundials are pointing north.

Independent Work
Hand out a copy of "Make Your Own Sundial" (p. 75) to each child. Help children cut out the gnomon and cut the slit in the base as indicated. Help them to fold the gnomon along the line and insert it into the base, making sure it is correctly oriented. They then need to secure it underneath with a strip of tape. Place the completed sundials in direct sunlight and use a compass to point them northward. Ask children to estimate the time from looking at their sundials. Compare their estimates with the correct time. If possible, repeat at a different time of day.

Support less-confident learners in making and reading their sundials. Challenge more-confident learners by asking why the time on the sundials might be different from the correct time, drawing out the limitations of the sundial.

Wrap-Up
Ask children to share their sundial experiences. Encourage them to judge the accuracy of the sundials and suggest their limitations.

Opaque vs. Transparent

Learning objectives
- To understand that opaque materials do not let light through and transparent materials let a lot of light through.
- To use knowledge about light and shadows to predict which materials will form a shadow, and to plan how to test this.
- To compare the shadows formed by different materials and to draw conclusions from their results.

Resources
- "Opaque vs. Transparent" Notebook file
- "Light, Shadows, and Materials" (p. 76)
- a collection of opaque, transparent (plastic bottles, acetate sheets), and translucent (fine gauze, thin nylon tights) objects
- flashlights or other more powerful light sources, such as an overhead projector
- large sheets of white card

Whiteboard tools
- Pen tray
- Spotlight tool
- Select tool

Getting Started
Position an object in front of the beam from the projector and ask children to discuss what they can see on the whiteboard. Review any previous work on shadow formation. Take care to avoid looking directly into the projector beam. Tell children that they will be using their knowledge of light and shadows to predict whether a collection of objects made from different materials will form a shadow when light is shone at them.

Mini-Lesson
1. Present children with the collection of objects and discuss what each is made from.

2. Display page 2 of the "Opaque vs. Transparent" Notebook file and ask children to predict which objects will form a shadow and which ones will not. Write the names of the materials in the appropriate frames.

3. Discuss how children could ensure a fair test by asking them what they are going to keep the same (light source; distance between light, object, and card), what they will change (object/material), and what they will measure (intensity of shadow).

Independent Work
Hand out a copy of "Light, Shadows, and Materials" (p. 76) to each child. Ask children to choose a number of objects and complete the first three columns of the sheet. Invite them to test the objects using the flashlights and white card, taking care to test in a fair manner. Tell children to record their findings in the next three columns, describing the shadow produced as *dark*, *pale*, or *none* and describing the object as *transparent*, *translucent*, or *opaque*.

Support less-confident learners in making and checking predictions. Challenge more-confident learners by asking them to provide reasons for their predictions in terms of what is happening to the light.

Wrap-Up
Classify children's findings by writing in the names of the objects in the appropriate frames on page 3 of the Notebook file. Discuss and then drag and drop each scientific term (*opaque*, *translucent*, *transparent*) over the appropriate frames. Tell children that they are going to be using this knowledge in an underwater adventure challenge.

Display page 4. Activate the Spotlight tool and go to the next page. Resize the spotlight to increase or decrease difficulty. Ask children to move the spotlight to find and identify all the animals on page 5. Exit the Spotlight tool and check their answers. Move the black net and the rock to reveal the two hidden creatures. Encourage children to classify each material using their learning from the lesson (water is transparent, net is translucent, and rock is opaque). Use page 6 to summarize what children have learned in this lesson.

Sounds Around Us

Learning objectives

- To know that there are many different sources of sounds.
- To explore sounds using the sense of hearing.
- To make observations of sounds by listening carefully.

Resources

- "Sounds Around Us" Notebook file
- large outline plan of the school and its grounds for each group

Whiteboard tools

- Pen tray
- Select tool

Getting Started

Display page 2 of the "Sounds Around Us" Notebook file. Ask children to recall the five senses. Write their answers on the SMART Board (hearing, sight, touch, taste, and smell). Invite them to identify which part of their body they use for each sense. Ask them which sense they would use for listening and then circle the relevant image on the page.

Go to page 3. Ask children to share sounds that they can describe and make—for example, laughing, clapping, whistling, and other sound effects. Write some of the sounds on the board in one color and words to describe them in a different color.

Mini-Lesson

1. Go to page 4 of the Notebook file. Tell children to look at the picture of the kitchen and to imagine what sounds they might hear. Invite them to describe and imitate the sounds and identify the source. Press the different images to hear the linked sounds. Circle each sound source.

2. Ask children to suggest other sounds that might be heard in a kitchen. They could imitate or describe the sound to the rest of the class to see if the other children can identify it.

3. Take children on a listening walk around the school. Visit different areas within the school (for example, the office, another classroom, the library, the playground). Encourage children to listen very carefully for different sounds.

4. On returning to the classroom, ask them to recall the different sounds they heard in the different areas and identify the sources of the sounds.

5. Write children's findings on page 5 of the Notebook file.

Independent Work

Hand out copies of a large plan of the school and its grounds. Ask children to work in groups to draw the sources of the sounds they heard in the different places on the listening walk. They could also add labels to identify or describe the sounds they heard.

Encourage less-confident learners to think of at least one sound and its source for each of the different areas of the school. Ask more-confident learners to work in pairs or individually, and to use varied vocabulary when describing their sounds.

Wrap-Up

Ask children questions about their sound maps. For example: *Which was the quietest or loudest place? Where did we hear lots of sounds? Which sound was the quietest?* Go to page 6 of the Notebook file and play the listening game. Tell children to close their eyes and concentrate on listening. Press on the star above each box and ask them to identify what is making the sound. Check to see if they are correct by rubbing out the question mark boxes using the Eraser from the Pen tray. Go to page 7. Ask children what they have found out or learned in today's lesson, and use the page to record their comments.

Making Sounds

Learning objectives

- To know that there are many different ways of making sounds.
- To present results and to interpret these.

Resources

- "Making Sounds" Notebook file
- "Sorting Musical Instruments" (p. 77)
- a picture of an orchestra
- a piece of orchestral music to play to children
- if possible, some orchestral instruments to show children
- a range of musical instruments that can be played by blowing, hitting, plucking, and shaking, for children to explore

Whiteboard tools

- Pen tray
- Select tool

Getting Started

Remind children of previous work, listening to the sounds in and around the school (see p. 44). Ask them to recall some of the sounds they heard and describe them using appropriate vocabulary—for example, *quiet, tapping, short.* Write their words on page 2 of the "Making Sounds" Notebook file, asking them to make sounds in the ways suggested.

Mini-Lesson

1. Explain to children that they will be investigating musical instruments to find different ways of making sounds.

2. Open page 3 of the Notebook file. Press a star and identify which instrument is making the sound. Ask for volunteers to drag the image of the instrument next to the correct star. Repeat for each of the stars.

3. Go to page 4. Explain that the different instruments make different sounds. Ask children if they know the names of any of the instruments and write in some of these. Play a piece of orchestral music and tell the class to listen out for different instruments.

4. Discuss the names of the instruments on page 5 and ask for volunteers to drag and drop the labels. If possible, have real examples of the instruments to show children. Ask them to imitate or describe the sounds made by the instruments. Compare this to the sound made by a real instrument.

5. Ask: *How do these instruments make their sounds; do you blow into them, hit them, pluck them, or shake them?*

Independent Work

Ask children to explore a range of musical instruments, finding out how each instrument makes its sound. They should group the instruments according to how they are played—for example, blowing, hitting, plucking, or shaking. Hand out copies of "Sorting Musical Instruments" (p. 77) for children to record their findings.

Allow less-confident learners plenty of hands-on experience with the instruments, and discuss with them the different ways they are producing the sounds. Encourage more-confident learners to label their drawings.

Wrap-Up

Go to page 6 of the Notebook file. Ask for volunteers to drag the images from the box at the foot of the page and drop them into the appropriate column in the table. Ask children questions about their results. For example: *Which group includes the most or least instruments? Are there any instruments that could belong to two groups?* Ask children what they have found out or learned from their exploration and record this on page 7 of the Notebook file.

Properties of Magnets

Learning objectives
- To know that there are forces between magnets and that magnets can attract (pull towards) and repel (push away from) each other.
- To make and record careful observations of magnets.
- To make generalizations about what happens when magnets are put together.

Resources
- "Properties of Magnets" Notebook file
- a variety of strong magnets of different sizes and shapes, some with the poles labeled

Whiteboard tools
- Pen tray
- Select tool
- Lines tool
- Delete button

Getting Started

Review children's knowledge of push and pull forces from previous lessons by asking them to describe or demonstrate examples of such forces (such as pushing a pencil, pulling open a door). Summarize what children know on page 2 of the "Properties of Magnets" Notebook file.

Mini-Lesson

1. Use pages 3 and 4 of the Notebook file to explain the legend of Sir Isaac Newton's discovery of gravity: *While resting under a tree, Sir Isaac Newton observed an apple falling from the tree. He realized there must be a pull force directly toward the center of the Earth that not only acted on apples and people, but on the moon as well.*

2. Compare this with the push force on page 5 when the ball is kicked. Use the Pen or Lines tools (select the arrows) to illustrate the direction of forces on pages 3 and 5.

3. Tell children that they are going to be investigating the properties of magnets and describing the forces they observe and feel.

4. Present them with the collection of different magnets and remind them not to drop them as it damages them.

Independent Work

Ask children to choose one pair of magnets at a time and put them very close together, observing and feeling what happens. Encourage children to explore different ways of putting the magnets together. Ensure that all children investigate the magnets that have the poles labeled. Keep page 6 of the Notebook file on display to remind children of their objective. Challenge children to try to discuss their observations in terms of push and pull forces.

Support less-confident learners in describing their investigations and observations clearly. Challenge more-confident learners by asking them to describe what is happening in terms of the two poles.

Wrap-Up

Ask children to describe what they observed with the unlabeled and labeled magnets. Look at the top two magnets on page 7 of the Notebook file. Ask children what they think would happen if they were dragged closer together. Ask them to write *push* or *pull force*. Introduce the term *attract*. Delete the top grey box to reveal the answer. Repeat for the bottom two magnets and introduce the term *repel*. Repeat a similar exercise for the magnets on page 8.

Go to page 9. Ask children to generalize about what happens when two magnets are put together using scientific terms (*push, pull, force, attract, repel*). Use the Eraser to reveal these words hidden in the box.

Magnetic Materials

Learning objectives

- To make and test predictions about whether or not materials are magnetic.
- To make careful observations.
- To know that magnets attract some metals but not others and that other materials are not attracted to magnets.
- To use results to draw conclusions, indicating whether predictions were accurate about which materials were magnetic.

Resources

- "Magnetic Materials" Notebook file
- strong magnets
- a collection of magnetic objects (made from iron, steel, cobalt, and nickel)
- a collection of nonmagnetic objects (including those made from gold, brass, copper, and aluminum)

Whiteboard tools

- Pen tray
- Select tool

Getting Started

Go to page 2 of the "Magnetic Materials" Notebook file. Recap any previous work on the properties of magnets—especially the force of attraction between opposite poles. Ensure that children are confident at using the terms *attract*, *attraction*, *repel*, and *repulsion*. Use the Eraser to reveal the key words hidden in the orange box.

Mini-Lesson

1. Play the simple game on page 3 of the Notebook file. Invite children to drag the objects to the wall to see which are magnetic. The nonmagnetic objects will disappear.

2. Talk about the materials from which the magnetic and nonmagnetic objects are made. Ask: *Are there any similarities between the materials?* Clarify that although an object may be attracted to a magnet, it is not necessarily a magnet itself.

3. Tell children that they are going to investigate a number of materials to discover whether or not the materials are magnetic (attracted to a magnet).

4. Display the resources and discuss how children could find out whether or not each object is magnetic. Consider together how to conduct the investigation fairly (using the same magnet/same number of magnets, and so on). Write children's ideas on page 4.

5. Ask children to make clear predictions.

Independent Work

Before testing, ask children to sort their objects into two groups: magnetic and nonmagnetic, based on their predictions. Ask them to test each object and sort them into two groups (magnetic and nonmagnetic), noting any objects that go against their predictions. Invite children to discuss what they have discovered (especially any surprises) and to make an appropriate generalization.

Support less-confident learners in their use of scientific language and be sure they know what is meant by a *magnetic material*. Extend the activity by asking children to give possible explanations for any surprises.

Wrap-Up

Display page 5 of the Notebook file and use children's results to write the names of the objects in the appropriate frame. Discuss what the results show. Establish that some objects that contain metal are magnetic and some are not. Ask children to make a general statement about what the results show (that magnets, and some, but not all, metals are magnetic materials) and write the conclusion in the frame. To extend the learning, write the names of the metals next to the appropriate objects and ask children to make an appropriate generalization (iron and steel are magnetic but aluminum, brass, copper, and gold are not). Use the multiple-choice "Magnets Quiz" (on page 6) to assess children's understanding of the properties of magnets and magnetic materials.

What Does Electricity Do?

Learning objective
- To know that everyday appliances use electricity (including things that light up, heat up, produce sounds, and move).

Resources
- "What Does Electricity Do?" Notebook file
- a variety of electrical appliances that use power cords and batteries
- old catalogs containing pictures of electrical appliances
- scissors
- glue
- paper
- individual whiteboards and pens

Whiteboard tools
- Pen tray
- Select tool

Getting Started
Show children a variety of electrical appliances (include some that use power cords and some that use batteries). Talk about what the appliances are and what they do. Ask children to consider what makes them work. Explain that they work because *electricity* gives them power. Ensure that children understand that electricity can come from a power outlet or from a battery. Ask them to decide what supplies the electricity that powers each object. Record their responses on page 2 of the "What Does Electricity Do?" Notebook file.

Mini-Lesson
1. Look again at the electrical appliances. Explain that electricity provides energy to an appliance in order to make it perform a specific function. For example, the electricity that goes to a lamp makes the bulb light up, meaning that the energy from the electricity is turned into light.

2. Ask children to consider what kind of output the energy from electricity can be turned into. (They should suggest heat, light, sound, and movement.)

3. Explain that some appliances turn the energy from electricity into more than one output. For example, a television turns electricity into light (for the picture) and sound.

4. Go to page 3 and open the "Uses of Electricity" interactive quiz. Ask children to decide what the main output of each appliance is. Some of the appliances may have more than one output, so ensure that children understand that they are looking for the main output only.

5. Use page 4 to summarize the answers to the quiz.

Independent Work
Provide each group with a selection of old catalogs, scissors, paper, and glue. Ask children to find and cut out pictures of things that use electricity from the catalogs. Encourage children to sort the pictures that they gather according to the main output of the object pictured—heat, light, sound, or movement. Allow children to choose their own way to record their decisions. Encourage more-confident learners to use Venn diagrams with intersecting circles to consider those appliances that have two outputs.

Wrap-Up
Take a sample of children's work and scan it into the computer. (Add scanned images of children's work to the page by selecting Insert, then Picture File, and browsing to where you have saved the images.) Display the work on page 5 of the Notebook file and ask children to comment on it. Annotate the work with some of children's comments. Ask: *Have the appliances been sorted correctly? Has the work been recorded in an easy-to-understand way?* Discuss any errors or misconceptions that may arise in children's work. As a final assessment, give children individual whiteboards and ask them questions about the appliances that they viewed earlier. For example: *How many of the appliances turn the energy from the electricity into heat? What output does the radio give?* Have children write their answers on their whiteboards.

Dangers of Electricity

Learning objectives
- To know that everyday appliances are connected to power lines and that they must be used safely.
- To know that some devices use batteries, which supply electricity; these can be handled safely.

Resources
- "Dangers of Electricity" Notebook file
- an electrical safety video*
- an electrical safety poster
- individual whiteboards and pens
- felt-tipped pens
- construction paper

Whiteboard tools
- Pen tray
- Select tool
- Highlighter pen

---

* Web sites featuring electrical safety videos for kids

http://www.snopud.com/Education/esafety/eswvideos.ashx?p=1721

http://www.safenotsorry.org/videos_ElectricalSafety18minutes.html

Getting Started

If available, watch a video about electrical safety together (see Resources). Discuss the dangers of electricity with children and answer any questions that they may have. Explain that electricity can be very useful as it allows us to see when it is dark (and watch television!). Stress that although it is useful, it is also deadly if it is not used safely.

Ask children what they think electricity looks like. Explain that it is actually invisible so it may still be there to hurt them even if they can't see it. Use page 2 of the "Dangers of Electricity" Notebook file to write notes.

Mini-Lesson

1. Give each child an individual whiteboard and ask children to write lists of appliances that use electricity that can be seen around the classroom. Ask them to write beside each appliance whether it is powered by battery or by power lines. Remind them that batteries supply only small amounts of electricity so they are safe for us to touch and use.

2. Invite children to share their answers. Make a note of their responses on page 3 of the Notebook file.

3. Next, ask children to take a close look at the picture displayed on page 4. Encourage them to talk to a partner about the electrical hazards that they can see in the picture.

4. Invite volunteers to come to the SMART Board to circle or highlight the hazards that they can see, and then talk about them as a class.

5. Display page 5. Ask: *Do you think the younger children in the school know about the dangers of electricity? How could you let them know?*

6. If available, show children an electrical safety poster and talk about its message and design.

Independent Work

Assign partners to act as "critical friends." Provide pairs with sheets of construction paper and some felt-tipped pens. Ask them to create a poster to inform the younger children in the school about the dangers of electricity. Encourage children to use simple text and big bold pictures to illustrate their messages. Stop children every few minutes and ask them to look at their partner's poster. Encourage the "critical friend" to point out some positive aspects of the poster and, most important, state whether the poster is communicating the desired message.

Wrap-Up

Take some samples of children's work and scan them into the computer. (Add scanned images of children's work to the page by selecting Insert, then Picture File, and then browsing to where you have saved the images.) Add the examples to page 5 of the Notebook file and ask the class to comment on them. Evaluate whether or not the posters communicate the desired message. Encourage positive comments from children and annotate the posters with them. As a final reminder, ask children to tell a partner three ways to stay safe around electricity. Record their observations on page 6.

Building a Circuit

Getting Started

Explain that in order to make a bulb light up you need a bulb, a battery, and wire. Open page 2 of the "Building a Circuit" Notebook file. Ask children to match the objects to the labels. Show them a real battery, bulb, and wire.

Mini-Lesson

1. Tell children that they are going to try to build a circuit to light a bulb. Explain the term *circuit* as a closed loop that electricity travels around.

2. Explain that after the circuit has been made, children are going to draw a diagram of it.

3. Remind children of the equipment they will be using to build the circuit, and ask them to suggest ideas for how it could be represented in a diagram. Use page 3 of the Notebook file to record their ideas.

Independent Work

Supply each pair of children with a number of batteries, bulbs, and wires and challenge them to light the bulb. Ensure that all of the equipment is functioning correctly before handing it out. Do not give out battery and bulb holders at first. Without these, children can see the path that the current takes more easily, particularly through the bulb. If children are struggling to make the connections between the wires and the battery or bulb, supply the holders as appropriate. Remind children about what was discussed earlier—that a complete circuit is needed to light a bulb. When the pairs have lit the bulb, ask children to record the circuit as a labeled diagram. Encourage them to think about how and why the bulb lights up when a circuit is made.

Wrap-Up

Invite a volunteer to use page 4 of the Notebook file to create a labeled diagram of the circuit they made. Make the circuit to test whether it lights a bulb and then compare it to the others that children created. Point out that all the circuits are a closed loop with no breaks in them. Listen to children's ideas about how and why the bulb lights up, then explain how the bulb actually lights. Ensure that children understand that electricity is made in the battery and then travels around the circuit in one direction towards the bulb. Point out that inside the bulb there is a thin piece of wire that the electricity squeezes through. The electricity gets very hot and it glows. After the electricity leaves the bulb it returns to the battery to get some more energy, completing the circuit.

Learning objectives

- To make a complete circuit using a battery, wires, and bulbs.
- To explore how to make a bulb light up, explaining what happened and using drawings to present results.

Resources

- "Building a Circuit" Notebook file
- flashlight bulbs or other small bulbs
- batteries
- insulated wires* (with insulation stripped off the ends)
- clothespins, tape, rubber bands (to hold bulb, wire, and battery in place, if necessary)
- paper
- pencils

Whiteboard tools

- Pen tray
- Select tool

*Instead of wire, you can also use 30cm x 30cm strips of aluminum foil, folded in half lengthwise for durability.

Testing Circuits

Learning objectives

- To know that an electrical device will not work if there is no battery or if there is a break in the circuit.
- To make and test predictions about circuits that will work.
- To explain what happened, drawing on their knowledge of circuits.

Resources

- "Testing Circuits" Notebook file
- "What Works?" (p. 78)
- bulbs
- batteries
- insulated wires* (with insulation stripped off the ends)
- clothespins, tape, rubber bands (to hold bulb, wire, and battery in place, if necessary)

Whiteboard tools

- Pen tray
- Select tool

Instead of wire, you can also use 30cm x 30cm strips of aluminum foil, folded in half lengthwise for durability.

Getting Started

Open page 2 of the "Testing Circuits" Notebook file. Review what children already know about circuits by asking them to create a circuit that will light a bulb. Show them a complete circuit with the bulb lit and ask them what they could do to make the bulb go out. Listen and respond to their ideas.

Point out that a battery has a positive and negative end. Explain that the electricity flows out of the negative end and into the positive end when it is placed in a circuit.

Mini-Lesson

1. Ask children to consider what a circuit needs in order to work. Remind them of the importance of having a closed circuit if a bulb is to light up. Record their ideas on page 3 of the Notebook file.

2. Go to page 4. Look at the different circuits with children and ask them to predict whether the bulbs will light or not. Encourage them to explain their predictions, using their knowledge of circuits. Ask them to write the voting letters (a or b) on their individual whiteboards, then take a tally of their votes.

3. Once children have finished voting, invite volunteers to come to the SMART Board to drag and drop the diagrams into the appropriate boxes.

4. Choose one of the circuits and ask children to explain how they could find out whether their prediction was correct or not. Elicit that they could make the circuit and see if the bulb lights.

5. Allow one of the children to make the circuit and test the prediction. Ask the rest of the class to explain why the circuit did or did not work, as appropriate.

Independent Work

Give each child a copy of "What Works?" (p. 78). Ask them to look at the picture of each bulb on the sheet and to record their prediction about whether or not it will light. Allow children access to bulbs, batteries, wires, and holders. Encourage them to build the circuits on the sheet to test their predictions. Tell them to use the sheet to record the results of their tests. Challenge children to explain why the bulb did or did not light. Ask them to record these ideas on the sheet. Encourage children to talk with a partner about their predictions and explanations.

Wrap-Up

Go through each problem on the reproducible sheet, one at a time, and ask children whether the bulb lit up or not. Use page 5 of the Notebook file to sort the images into the appropriate columns. Encourage children to give an explanation for each problem. Address any errors or misconceptions they may have along the way.

Rocks Everywhere!

Learning objectives
- To understand that rocks are used for a variety of purposes.
- To understand that rocks are chosen for particular purposes because of their characteristics.

Resources
- "Rocks Everywhere" Notebook file
- notebooks and pens

Whiteboard tools
- Pen tray
- Select tool
- Highlighter pen

Getting Started

Ask children to point out any obvious uses of stone or rock in the classroom or nearby. Make a distinction between naturally occurring rocks, such as slate or granite, and manmade materials that contain rock, such as tarmac and concrete. Write children's ideas and responses on page 2 of the "Rocks Everywhere" Notebook file.

Mini-Lesson

1. Read and discuss the sentences on pages 3 and 4 of the Notebook file. Are children surprised by any of the facts?

2. Highlight anything interesting and annotate any questions that children have about rocks.

3. Ask for any further examples of rocks used in the home.

4. Encourage children to think about what rock the objects are made from and the reason a particular rock has been used.

5. Invite individual children to highlight the key words to identify all the rocks' names and associated technical vocabulary.

Independent Work

Organize children to carry out a survey of the school buildings and playground to identify where rocks have been used. Ask them to jot down where they identify a rock has been used and why it has been chosen (for example, steps made from granite because it does not wear away easily). Ask children to consider whether the rock is natural or a manmade material. Encourage them to record their data in a table. Suggest column headings such as: *What is it? What is it made from? Why was this rock used? Is it manmade or natural?*

Wrap-Up

Come together back in class and discuss what children have discovered. Write their responses on page 5 of the Notebook file. Ask: *Do any of the rocks have common features? Are there any rocks that you would like to find out more about?* Display page 6 and ask children if they can remember the facts they learned at the beginning of the lesson. Invite individual children to come to the board and drag and drop the cards so that each phrase fits with the correct sentence starter. Check against pages 3 and 4 to ensure that the phrases have been correctly matched.

Soils

Learning objectives

- To understand that beneath all of the Earth's surfaces there is rock.
- To understand that there are different kinds of soil depending on the rock from which they come.

Resources

- "Soils" Notebook file
- tall, straight-sided, clear glass containers with tight lids, such as tall jelly jars
- large quantities of three topsoils from different locations
- water

Whiteboard tools

- Pen tray
- Select tool
- Screen Shade
- Shapes tool
- Fill Color tool
- Pen tool

Getting Started

Open the "Soils" Notebook file and go to page 2. Discuss children's own experiences of digging in a garden. Find out if any of them have noticed any differences or made any discoveries about the feel or appearance of the soil as they have dug deeper. Ask: *What do you think is underneath the soil?*

Mini-Lesson

1. Display page 3 of the Notebook file and tell children that they will be looking at a number of pictures that involve rock.

2. Move through pages 4 to 9 of the Notebook file and, in each case, ask children to identify where any rock is located. Draw out that, even if it is not visible, there is always solid rock underneath the surface vegetation, buildings, or soil. Pull the tabs to reveal more information about each picture.

3. Move on to page 10. Pull down the Screen Shade to gradually reveal a soil profile. Discuss the profile layer by layer from the top. Elicit that most people would not have experienced digging deeper than the topsoil.

4. Go to page 11 and explain that the labels have been mixed up. Children have to drag and drop them back into their correct positions.

5. Display and discuss page 12. Explain that children are going to investigate the contents of a number of soils by separating the materials within the soils.

Independent Work

Divide the class into small groups. Invite each group to fill a glass container halfway with one of the soils, and carefully add enough water so that the container is three-quarters full. (**Safety note:** Refer to your school's health and safety guidelines when handling soils.) Ask children to close the lid tightly and then shake the container well for one or two minutes, or until the soil is fully suspended in the water. Have them store their container in a dark, undisturbed place. Discuss what children think will happen. Wait 24 hours and check if the soil particles have fully settled. (There will be a layer of clear water on top of the settled bands of soil.) Once the soil particles have settled, ask children to study, draw, and label the container and its contents carefully. Ensure that children move the containers with care so that particles do not enter into the solution again.

Wrap-Up

Discuss children's findings (from the bottom upwards, individual bands of settled sand, silt, clay, organic matter, and water might be visible). Display page 13 of the Notebook file and invite children to draw and place colored rectangles on the containers to represent, as accurately as possible, the settled bands for the three different soils. (They could use the Shapes and the Fill Color tools to do this, or use the Pen tool, selecting different colors and thick settings.) Discuss any differences in the layering and draw out the fact that all soils contain different amounts of sand, silt, clay, and organic matter and that the quantities involved usually depend on the parent rock that is underneath the soil. Write this conclusion on page 14.

Investigation: Water Flow

Learning objectives

- To use simple tools to measure volumes of liquids and to measure time.
- To use results to make comparisons and to draw and explain conclusions.

Resources

- "Investigation: Water Flow" Notebook file
- "Investigation Planning" (p. 74)
- "Water Flow Investigation" (p. 79)
- sticky labels
- stopwatches
- measuring cups
- large trays
- different soil types (sand, clay, loam, and so on)
- two-liter plastic bottles, one for each group of children
- sharp scissors

Whiteboard tools

- Pen tray
- Select tool
- On-screen Keyboard

(Microsoft Excel is required to view the embedded spreadsheet in the Notebook file.)

Before You Start

Cut the tops off the bottles, about one quarter of the way down from the neck. Make a few small holes in the base of each bottle. Place the cut-off necks upside down in the top of the bottles to act as funnels.

Getting Started

Ask children to describe what happens to the water when a wave rolls up a sandy beach. Discuss why the sand seems to "dry out" so quickly when the wave retreats (the water quickly flows down between the sand particles). Go to page 2 of the "Investigation: Water Flow" Notebook file and draw a diagram to help children visualize what is happening.

Ask children about their experiences of water sinking into soil (for example, when they water potted plants). Go to page 3 and tell children that there are six main soil types (sandy, silty, clay, peaty, chalky, and loamy). Explain that they will be testing some (or all) of them to find out how quickly water flows through each type.

Mini-Lesson

1. Discuss how children could find out how fast water travels through each soil type. Establish how this could be planned as an investigation, including the resources they would need.

2. Using page 4 of the Notebook file, discuss how children could make the test fair, by asking them what they are going to keep the same (volume of water), what they will change (soil type), and what they will measure (how long the water takes to flow through the soil and start dripping from the bottle). Write these points on the page or drag the phrases from the word bank.

3. Ask children to complete their own copies of the "Investigation Planning" sheet (p. 74).

Independent Work

Divide the class into small groups. Hand out copies of the "Water Flow Investigation" sheet (p. 79). Ask each group to fill a plastic bottle a quarter of the way with one of the soil types, remembering to label it, and replace the cut-off neck. Tell children to hold the bottles over the trays and pour 250ml of water onto the soil, ensuring that they start timing immediately. They must stop timing when the water starts dripping from the holes in the base of the bottle. Ask them to record the time on their sheets. Repeat this process with a number of soil types.

Wrap-Up

Discuss children's results. Explain that bar graphs can be used to present results clearly, so that comparisons can be made more easily. Press the hyperlinked button on page 5 of the Notebook file to open the "Water Flow Investigations" spreadsheet. Use the On-screen Keyboard to enter children's data in the table. Discuss the resulting bar graph, using it to explain which soil type the water flowed through the most quickly. Talk about the reasons for this (sand drains quickly because of the spaces between particles, whereas clay drains poorly due to few air spaces). Compare the results with their predictions. Use page 6 to summarize what they have learned.

Label the Body Parts

Label the parts of the human body.

Use these words to help you.

WORD BANK

arm	head	elbow	nose	shoulder	waist
ear	knee	foot	neck	hand	leg
eye	chest	hip	toes	mouth	

Science Lessons for the SMART Board: Grades 1–3 © 2011, Scholastic

Food Diary

Write in the foods that you ate today.

breakfast	
lunch	
dinner	
snack	

Food Groups

Use your own food diary to create a tally chart of the different types of food you have eaten.

Food group	Tally
Meat, fish, and eggs	
Fruits and vegetables	
Cereals, bread, and grains	
Dairy	
Sugar and fats	

Use the tally chart you have made to create a bar graph of the different types of food you have eaten.

	Meat, fish, and eggs	Fruits and vegetables	Cereals, bread, and grains	Dairy	Sugar and fats
10					
9					
8					
7					
6					
5					
4					
3					
2					
1					

Science Lessons for the SMART Board: Grades 1–3 © 2011, Scholastic

Investigating Differences, Part 1

Measure the height and foot length of five people.
Record your results in these tables.

Name	Height in cm

Name	Foot length in cm

Does the tallest person have the longest feet?

_____

Science Lessons for the SMART Board: Grades 1–3 © 2011, Scholastic

Investigating Differences, Part 2

Use your results to complete this bar graph.

Foot length in cm

26				
25				
24				
23				
22				
21				
20				
19				
18				
17				
16				
15				
14				
13				
12				
11				
10				
9				
8				
7				
6				
5				
4				
3				
2				
1				

Height in cm (shortest to tallest)

Science Lessons for the SMART Board: Grades 1–3 © 2011, Scholastic

Plant Investigations

Growth investigation: Number of leaves

Where will the plants be kept?

How much water and when?

What will we measure and when?

Growth investigation: Water

Where will the plants be kept?

How much water and when?

What will we measure and when?

Growth investigation: Light

Where will the plants be kept?

How much water and when?

What will we measure and when?

WORD BANK

light	height	ruler	same
dark	stem	tape measure	different
sunlight	soil	color	amount
shady	hours	description	every
milliliters (ml)	days	health	quantity

Science Lessons for the SMART Board: Grades 1–3 © 2011, Scholastic

Science Lessons for the SMART Board: Grades 1–3 © 2011, Scholastic

Name _____

Date _____

Stem Observation

When your teacher tells you, carefully draw the setup in each box showing what happens to the colored water.

Time

Time

Time

Match the Animals

Draw lines to match each adult animal with its young.

Science Lessons for the SMART Board: Grades 1–3 © 2011, Scholastic

Animal Diets

Use these tables to help you carry out your animal diets survey.

Name of animal	✓
Has this animal ever eaten:	

Name of animal	✓
Has this animal ever eaten:	

Science Lessons for the SMART Board: Grades 1–3 © 2011, Scholastic

Identifying and Describing Materials

Choose three objects. Identify and describe what they are made from.

Draw an object here	This is a _____ It is made from _____ It is _____ _____ _____
Draw an object here	This is a _____ It is made from _____ It is _____ _____ _____
Draw an object here	This is a _____ It is made from _____ It is _____ _____ _____

Science Lessons for the SMART Board: Grades 1–3 © 2011, Scholastic

Twist and Stretch!

	squash?	bend?	twist?	stretch?	return to original state?
play dough					
elastic band					
pebble					
clay					
foam ball					

Putting on the Heat

Predict what will happen when you hold each of the candies in your hand for
3 minutes. Try it and see what happens.

Name or type of candy	What do you think will happen when you hold it?	What actually happened when you held it?

Think of other materials that will change when they are heated. How will they change?

1. _____   _____

2. _____   _____

3. _____   _____

4. _____   _____

5. _____   _____

Science Lessons for the SMART Board: Grades 1–3 © 2011, Scholastic

What Are the Properties?

Sketch	Name of material	Describe the properties of this material

── WORD BANK ──

fragile	crumbly	elastic	tough	irregular
hard	coarse	flimsy	durable	squashy
smooth	regular	delicate	inflexible	powdery
transparent	solid	weak	clear	firm
flexible	brittle	sturdy	stretchy	frail
rough	silky	stiff	bendable	glossy
soft	spongy	rigid	bumpy	shiny

Stretching Investigation

Name of tights	Thickness (least thick to thickest)	Length before stretching (cm)	My prediction (most stretchy to least stretchy)	Length when stretched (cm)

Pushes and Pulls Around the House

Find things in your house that are moved by pushing or pulling.
Draw them in the boxes.

Things moved by pushing	Things moved by pulling

Vehicle Test

Vehicle	Distance traveled in cm

Label the axes.

Bar graph _____

Science Lessons for the SMART Board: Grades 1–3 © 2011, Scholastic

Ramp Height

Height of ramp	Distance traveled in cm

Label
the
axes.

Bar graph _____

Light Sources Around the House

Find six **sources of light** in or around your house. Draw them in the boxes.

Science Lessons for the SMART Board: Grades 1–3 © 2011, Scholastic

Name _____

Date _____

Shadow Investigation

Use a ruler to draw on lines of light from the light source to the board. Don't forget that some light is blocked by the object!

Draw the shadow on the whiteboard here.

Draw the object here.

Draw the light source here.

Describe what is happening. Use these words to help you:

light　　source　　straight　　travel　　block　　shadow　　form　　line

Investigation Planning

PLANNING

What are you trying to find out?
(A question that can be tested)

What do you think will happen?
(Prediction)

What will you use? (Resources)

LABELED DIAGRAM

FAIR TESTING

What will you change?
(The variable we are testing)

What will you keep the same?
(Variables that will be kept constant)

What will you measure and record? (Results)

Science Lessons for the SMART Board: Grades 1–3 © 2011, Scholastic

Make Your Own Sundial

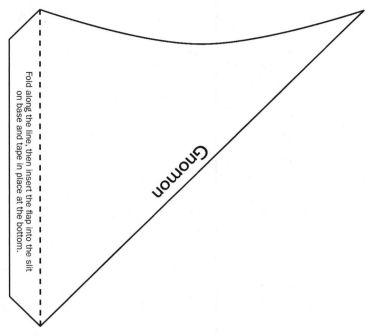

Fold along the line, then insert the flap into the slit on base and tape in place at the bottom.

Gnomon

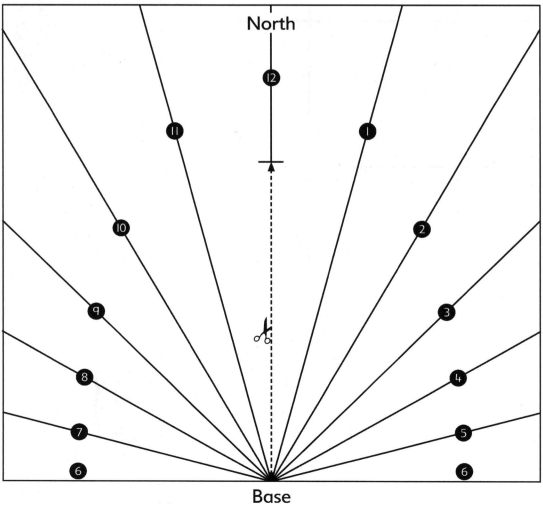

North

12

11   1

10   2

9   3

8   4

7   5

6   6

Base

Light, Shadows, and Materials

Complete the first three columns before you begin your investigation.
Record your investigation results in the last three columns.

Object	Material	Prediction (all light, some light, no light)	Shadow (none, pale, dark)	Correct prediction? (yes, no)	Transparent, translucent, or opaque?

Science Lessons for the SMART Board: Grades 1–3 © 2011, Scholastic

Sorting Musical Instruments

Look at some musical instruments. How do you make a sound with each one?
Draw the instruments in the correct boxes.

Blow	Hit
Pluck	**Shake**

What Works?

Circuit	Prediction Will it work? (Yes/No)	Result Did it work? (Yes/No)	Explanation Why did this happen?

Water Flow Investigation

Soil type	Time (seconds)

Remember: 60 seconds = 1 minute
120 seconds = 2 minutes
180 seconds = 3 minutes

Notes

Science Lessons for the SMART Board: Grades 1–3 © 2011, Scholastic